Single and Sober:

Who Found My Slipper?

Karen Foley

Karen Foley

DEDICATION

This book is dedicated to my son, Jesse Vieira. He motivates me to be the best person I can be and is my inspiration for leaving the world a better place.

"If you'd like to read an insightful journey about personal growth as well as looking for a soulmate, then sit down with this book. Karen's self-evaluation and search for understanding helps us understand ourselves, too."
-Mary Dessein, author of *When I Was a Rock Star: Thoughts on Being Present in the World;* available in paperback and e-book on Amazon. Mary's creative blog is at www.marydessein.com

SPECIAL THANKS TO

Ann Patrice Foley, Dave Darling, Patrice Foley, Kitty Foley, Aunt Pat Foley, Dan Fox, Jesse Vieira, Emma Klonoski, Elsie Pray, Jerry Pray, Mary Dessein, Verna Doherty, Rebekah Reineke, S. O. Terra, Sara Leinen, Terry Davis, Jennifer Taylor, Jennifer Cook, Devin Rice, Lupita Ruelas, Joan Norton, Lauren Marie, Matthew Buza, Toni Kief, and the Writers Cooperative of the Pacific Northwest. Without each of you I would not have been able to open my laptop and finish drafting this book. Thanks to all the men I dated who were kind and courageous as well as those who contributed to creating memorable material to move this manuscript into matter. Thanks to all for helping me grow.

TABLE OF CONTENTS

1 TEDDY – SEPTEMBER 1979

I met Teddy when I was twenty. He was dressed as a gorgeous female coming out of that shack town shanty I was renting in the suburbs of Detroit. I had never met someone that was out and out gay in the late seventies, let alone dressed as a Drag Queen. "Bombshell Barbie" they called her, quite famous in the greater Detroit/Ann Arbor area at the time. I was immediately drawn to his electric energy and ways, his wild spirit, his zest for life. I connected with him as a party animal friend and as a human being.

Teddy and his family were from Tennessee before moving to the suburbs of Detroit when he was in grade school. His family did not accept having a feminine boy in the family and rejected him during his childhood. He talked about being called "Sally" by family and friends all the while seeking his parents and big brother's approval. Instead, he was compared to his "normal" heterosexual brother never quite living up to the challenge. He didn't like sports and did not work on cars.

Teddy's father would cut him down, his brother ragged him and didn't stand up for him at school, and his mother tried to make up for it by purchasing gifts for him. She taught him that money was what mattered, not time or affection, not acceptance or kindness. He learned to buy for himself and buy for others to show and receive love. I never met anyone so generous with their money; he always played the big shot. Teddy picked up the tab everywhere he went, no matter if he knew the people or not, and he drew people near him who took total advantage of him. He desperately wanted to be loved and accepted.

One of my earliest memories of Teddy was getting drunk at Mr. Mikes Bar and Grill in Westland, MI, and going to his house in Inkster after the bar closed with a dozen or so others. It was my twentieth birthday; I was very drunk. Teddy took me into his dressing room surrounded by ball gowns. He taped up my breasts turning my A cup bosom into a C cup, at least for appearance's sake. I was amazed by his talent and fell in love with Teddy right then and there.

This was not in the traditional sense, our love for one another has always been platonic, but it has also been deep. For the next dozen years, we were vacation buddies. When I left Detroit and moved to St. Petersburg, FL, Teddy came to visit. We played hard. I came back to Michigan to visit my family, and he was always part of the scene. Trip after trip home he would show up with his latest sports car and hand me the keys for the duration of my stay. My family loved him so much that we adopted him as part of the Foley family and gave him a gold "F" charm necklace that he forever cherished.

Then, in the early nineties, Teddy came to see me after I moved to WA. He had gotten clean and sober. I was still a freaking mess, close to hitting my bottom. I was hooked on Methamphetamine, called "Crank" at the time, hanging out and working at the bar. While I told him I'd go to 12-Step meetings with him before he arrived, it was six months prior to my getting clean and I wasn't ready for recovery support. Instead, I took him to all the bars; the one I worked at, the one my boyfriend Chase worked at, and the ones we partied and played darts at. He went to AA meetings while we were working, then we brought the party home to play darts and party all night after our bars closed.

I felt horrible about putting Teddy through that later when I stopped drinking and using drugs. I realized then what I'd done to him when he only had six months sober was selfish and mean. I felt embarrassed. It was a big motivation that helped me stay sober. It was one of those awful times I wasn't proud of. I didn't want to forget, as it is important to be reminded of how blind and inconsiderate of others I was when actively drinking or using other drugs.

Teddy put up with a lot from me when he was sober, and I was not. I had no idea the table would turn years later. I only knew I was not a good friend to him during that trip. I brought the party home, took him to the bars, and didn't go to meetings with him as I had promised to do before he came to visit me in Washington.

When I finally got sober, I talked to Teddy a lot. We reconnected at a different level, and he was so glad when I got on board with my sobriety. He knew I needed it, and I wasn't getting support from my lover/soulmate/drug dealer/father of my baby who told me I should "save the treatment slot for someone who needed it" as we neglected our baby.

Teddy was my support. I loved him even deeper. When I celebrated my first year in recovery in 1993, he flew from Detroit to Seattle to give me my one-year coin, a very special token in the recovery rooms. That was so awesome. We stayed in touch and supported each other's new way of life. When I celebrated three years of recovery, he flew out again to give me my coin. He said he had four-years sober then; however, I believe he was dabbling into Xanax at the time, and probably abusing it. By the time I was five years clean and sober he flew out again, but he got drunk as a skunk while visiting and I felt embarrassed for him.

About that time, we parted ways for a period. He would call every year or two with thirty days sober again. Once when I was traveling, he called while on vacation in Tennessee with his meth making cousin. He was so cranked up that I tried to get him off the phone for over an hour and he was unable to notice or stop talking.

However, Teddy knew where to turn when he got ready to stop the party. He worked with me on the phone for three months solid as he lost his second job for addict type behaviors. He went from using drugs at work, to just smoking crack daily, to only using Xanax as prescribed, with an occasional slip-on alcohol. It was progress, not perfection.

He decided to come to WA for a couple weeks to try to get clean and sober and begin his life over again. I was excited he was coming to visit again, but I set up strict boundaries for his visit, too. I shouldn't have been surprised when he got off the plane loaded, having talked to him daily for three months. He knew he'd have to go to a hotel if he was using drugs or drinking.

I was embarrassed as I brought my son to the airport with me to pick him up. Teddy's always been my son's "Fun, crazy, rich, uncle" who loved him like his own.

Teddy came stumbling off that plane saying he took some Xanax to calm his nerves about flying but neglected to say he'd also taken someone else's suboxone.

I took him to a meeting where he surrendered the rest of that drug and I disposed of the suboxone strips in the toilet at an Alano Club overlooking Puget Sound. The meeting was about surrender, and we both needed that. I just couldn't put him in a hotel even though the decision to bring him to the guest room in my home went against my best moral judgment. My house has always been my sanctuary with no drugs or alcohol allowed. I don't allow newcomers with less than thirty days to visit my home. While I knew Teddy was high the night he arrived, I didn't expect him to continue using since we planned to attend meetings every day of his visit. That would have surely ruined my buzz.

I had a hard time sending Teddy to a hotel because of our history. He showed his love for me and my son through gifts, money, and attention repeatedly for decades. Even though I didn't take advantage of him, I felt an obligation to take care of him in his darkest hour. He never gave up on me…so I let him stay in my home despite our prearranged deal. He knew he couldn't stay with me if he was using drugs, and I backed out of our deal when he showed up loaded. I need al-anon.

We spent the next two solid weeks at 12-Step meetings every day. Toward the end of the trip at my cousin's house in the country, he came clean about the drugs he'd been taking daily since arriving. He gave up the pills, surrendered deeper, and wanted to stay another couple of weeks to get a little more time under his belt before going back to his using environment. We changed his phone number, got rid of his contacts, let his dealers know he is clean and sober and no longer reachable, and discussed his plan to taper off the Xanax he'd been on for most of the past thirty years.

Teddy was so electric, coming back into his authentic self. We love each other so much and we both were thrilled to have each other back. It is like having a sibling that likes and respects you, without competition or other sick family dynamics. True, pure love. We buy each other gifts and praise our near forty-year friendship as the treasure that it is. We laugh and go on Starbucks binges. He attends my home group, makes his usual grandiose impression, and falls in love with all my friends as they do him. He invites my friends out to dinner after the meetings and it brings me closer to my own circle of support. They love him, I love him, you can't help but love Teddy. He is dynamic, entertaining, electric, generous, and giving. He gave one of my friends a $100 bill to help fix her car and he bought fifteen of my friends the best ribs in town. He left a memory that people would surely talk about years later.

Teddy left me his humongous diamond ring since he knew I was coming to Detroit six months later for my sister's wedding. He figured if I invested three months on the phone this summer and then five weeks in person of personal addiction counseling services for him (his perception, not mine) that if he didn't make it six months sober, I was to keep the diamond ring. I had no intention of doing that.

Six months later I went to Detroit for my sister's wedding and Teddy was still doing awesome. He was four months at a new job. He hosted my family for the first time ever, letting us crowd his house with out-of-towners for the wedding. He let my son and nephew stay in his basement, and he let all my younger relatives party in his basement (not the brightest plan). He was an incredible host, friend, and brother.

He wanted me to come move in with him and date my new friend Don so I could get to know him better. I felt loved by Teddy and grateful to have him in my life. Teddy's different when he's sober. I told him I'd think about moving in with him if things between Don and I progressed to that point. I am very grateful he is back, my buddy, my friend, my confidant. I brought him his big fancy diamond ring, and he proudly accepted it back.

The week after I left, Teddy relapsed. At first, he was taking drugs from his nursing home job. Then he was drinking. Eventually he started smoking crack again and acting the fool on our phone calls. He was desperate, delusional, telling himself lies and believing them.

Sometimes I think Teddy and I were meant to have each other since we both spent our lives single, and we share love for my son as if we co-parented him. But then I lose hope in humankind, in beating this disease, in my buddy, Teddy. I begin to believe sobriety is just a joke. He's using drugs, I'm gambling and eating sugar on and off, and I'm using caffeine like there's no tomorrow. I start to question if it is possible to get clean and sober and remain healthy through time.

I'm losing hope about my own sobriety. I just want to check out emotionally as I hate how I am feeling. I am disappointed, hopeless, and doing things that I don't want to be doing. Knowing the insanity of this disease, I still hang out at the casino, spend money I don't want to spend, and stay hours longer than I intend. Every time I quit; I am determined not to return. Then I return. A little more beaten, a little more hopeless, and further from the belief I could stop and stay stopped.

I had a work trip that took me to Michigan. The day before I arrived in Detroit, Teddy started gambling again. He wasn't drinking and was proud of that. He was trying to get to the hotel to come see me, but he found himself stuck at the Casino nearby. It was within sight of the fancy downtown hotel where I stayed for work, but I doubted that I'd see my friend if I didn't chase him down.

I said "F-it" to my gambling addiction. I was two months abstinent from gambling and he insisted on meeting at the Casino. My addict within was okay with this plan and I wasn't resistant. I relapsed from gambling for the next two days and miraculously got back on track after that weekend. I did not realize it wouldn't be the last time I quit gambling. I don't know how I stopped long enough to meet up with the group of bosses and colleagues I travelled with. Still, I was playing with fire and Teddy was lighting the match. Teddy introduced me to the VIP room where only the hi-rollers/spenders go that lose multiple thousands of dollars with each spin. I didn't try it, but knowing it existed made me think about having to one day mortgage my house.

Within a few months and a few phone calls, Teddy started drinking again and became suicidal over gambling. He decompensated quickly. He lost his will to stop using and be present in his life. I can't stand talking to him on the phone, his filter is lifted, and he is inappropriate. He is a sloppy drunk, sometimes mean. He had 'friended' all my recovery friends on Facebook and he began to post things that were outrageous. The most recent post was a naked man, overweight, satisfying himself while dancing with his back to the camera. It was so gross, I was embarrassed to know him, let alone introduce him to my entire recovery world. I unfriended him on Facebook, but I don't think he noticed.

Teddy, my dear friend I've known for thirty-eight years, I love you, but I have got to let you go. I will continue to love you, from a distance.

UPDATE: SEPTEMBER 2016

I spent three more hours on the phone with Teddy. This was becoming routine and exhausting. He admitted he was using opiates now and had sworn to himself he'd never do that. He is desperately in need of help and could not see it. Denial is an amazing thing.

Teddy told me he was put on life support yesterday. He was so proud he used to be a nurse who worked at that same hospital in the ER. He bragged about un-intubating himself and how he walked out against medical advice. "I came home and got on the ladder and cleaned my windows, ha-ha", he squealed with delight. "Teddy, you died. When is enough going to be enough?", I asked.

I set a new boundary I'd never done before. I told him I could not continue our conversations if he was using. He was going to die, and I could not watch him kill himself. There was a change in the conversation at that moment where he seemed to wake up and notice that this was life or death. Eventually, he asked for my help getting into treatment. He was so scared of having to give up the benzos. I reassured him he'd have a doctor monitored detox and he would be okay. He finally surrendered to getting help. We worked together finding out where he could go based on his insurance. He took down the numbers. He decided to get clean, again.

It was Saturday night late into September 2016. He was found dead by his roommate on Sunday. The phone numbers were on his bedside table along with a note to his roommate to wake him up Monday because he was going to treatment. Then the withdrawal sets in. "One last hurrah" likely went through his head. I was glad I'd sent him sixty roses for his 60th birthday. He died much too young, and it was preventable. I saw it coming.

I heard the news from his mother who I'd only met for the first time the summer before. Teddy was proposing to me over that last year regularly and would not take no for an answer. He even announced he was getting married to his family at a backyard BBQ while he was on a date with the dude who was selling him narcotics. Their family and his date were shocked when he announced he was going to marry me.

Teddy wanted to become my husband because he had great health insurance for life, and he wanted me to have it. Plus, he wanted to move to WA and enjoy his senior years with me. I told him he was too much of a risk for me to marry due to his gambling, and other active addictions. He was surprised as he prided himself in making good money and paying his bills. Making good money was his blessing and his curse. I couldn't take the chance of ruining my credit, taking on his illness as a project to fix, nor bringing the chaos home. I did think about it though. I loved him.

Thank you, Teddy, for your generous spirit and thirty-eight-year friendship. I love and miss you with all my heart. Thank you for being in my life and helping me raise my son.

Thanks for being "Uncle Teddy", the one and only big personality I will forever know loved me. I would have married you for your insurance had you not been so incredibly toxic. I loved you always, in all ways, but even more when you were clean and sober. Your kind spirit and love will always have a sacred place in my heart. Rest in peace my dear friend.

2 DARREN – OCTOBER 2015

Tonight was so incredible. A romantic setting in the quaint Marysville restaurant, Frozo's, owned by an adorable couple. The Greek Lemon Pepper Chicken with Mizithra Spaghetti is scrumptious as always. I've eaten here at least a half dozen times and have never been disappointed. I prefer more contemporary décor, but this restaurant, filled with antiques, art from the 1920's, and the ambience, is cozy and classy. It seems to prepare the palette for authentic exquisite foods from the other side of the globe.

I am excited to see my friend, Darren. He has always had a crush on me, but he knows I don't feel the same. I do care about him, but I don't find him romantically attractive. It's been nice to talk about these things, so there are no resentments or unmet expectations. Last year, when he let me know about the crush he had on me, I gently, but clearly, let him know I only wanted to be friends. I do not feel the same electric feelings he seems to have toward me. I continue to pick him up to take him to our 12-Step recovery meetings after his doctor made him stop driving because of his medical condition.

There was one incident that changed my behavior around Darren. Six months ago, he made a comment about my being his girlfriend, so I immediately put the quash on that. I called him and asked if there was anything I'd said or done that gave him the impression I was his girlfriend? He blew this off as kidding, but I sensed he was not. I quit picking Darren up to drive him to the meeting because I did not want to lead him on. I have grown fond of him as a friend. Darren has been so sick since that time. He was able to get the surgery he long awaited to sustain his life. He claims he's used his nine lives with near death experiences waiting to qualify for surgery.

Darren texted me as he went through his ordeal, which included at least a half dozen hospitalizations, a big surgery, a nearly rejected organ, and finally, his recovery. I can be a cheerleader, but I don't visit him. I feel compassion for Darren, but I refuse to hang out at hospitals for him or most other acquaintances. I save those kinds of difficult visits for my closest family members only.

I do not choose to hang out at stinky, sterile hospitals unless the patient is in my inner circle. I hate hospitals, since both of my siblings who died, did so in these institutions. I was able to hold both of their hands as they took their last breaths, something I will forever appreciate, but the air smelt of death, and the environment was filled with sadness and suffering. I lose hope walking in those cold corridors and avoid going into them whenever possible.

Tonight, I headed out to dinner at a restaurant alone, thinking about how Darren was doing. I thought it would be nice to drive him to his favorite restaurant since he still can't drive, and he's been cooped up at home recovering for the past month. When I called, he had plans to order pizza for his adult children that were home, but he dropped his plans to come out with me. How sweet. He doesn't claim to hide his admiration, but at least he doesn't expect anything. The bone I am throwing him is a bit small, and a bit late, since he almost died nine times since I've picked him up and driven him to a meeting. I am clear about just being a friend, and a not-so-good friend at that, who never even visited him in the hospital and never mentioned why.

I knew Frozo's would be great to lift Darren's spirits, and mine too. I love to reconnect with old friends, and the fabulous food and atmosphere is a bonus compared to eating alone, which I have done enough of for a lifetime. I am feeling good, and I'm grateful to break bread with my friend from the fellowship. I could have invited a girlfriend and sponsee, Debra, but she is usually an hour or two late, and that drives me crazy, especially when I'm hungry. I am glad to have called Darren and that he is available. I will go out to dinner alone, but I'd prefer to eat with a friend. He was the perfect choice as he needed to leave his house and I wanted a companion for dinner.

I am all ears when Darren reports he has something serious to talk to me about. I sit in stillness and meet his intensity, returning his serious stare, entirely present. After having sat at my sister's bedside as she passed, and my brother's too, I am ready to hear his end-of-life enlightening moments with his near-death experiences. I can have those tough to talk about mortality conversations, which I expect he is about to share. Leaning forward, I listen with all the senses in my body for what is to come next.

"Since I have been given a new lease on life and I am going to live, I want to share the rest of my life with you, Karen. I am ready. If you don't think I'm too old, I want to share my life with you for the rest of my days, and I'm happy to say I'm going to live a long time now."

Gulp. I am stunned. How did we come to this moment? Has he not heard me the last three, four, or was it five times I told him I was not interested in him in that way? I am touched that he considers me a potential life partner and flattered that he continues to think of me as that special, but I am so embarrassed for him. I do not want to crush his spirit or hurt his feelings, but we've never even been on a date.

However, I start to feel irritated by his behavior. It is as if how I feel does not matter and my words are meaningless to him. I am picking up on the possibility that he has decided a woman who says no really means yes. Like his is the only opinion that matters in this equation. I begin to get mad, and I want to leave the restaurant.

He continues to tell me how he prayed about it. He says he asked his dead wife if it was okay, and she said, "Yes, go for it". It's too bad he didn't consult me. We've never even been on a date.

I tell Darren "I'm honored, but I don't feel the same". Just to pound in the point, I let him know I am seeking a man in his fifties. Darren is in his late sixties, but he looks and acts much older. He is a staunch Republican, proud of his career in the Military, and good at giving orders. I am fifty-six, but I've been told I look fifty and feel thirty-five. I am a left winged Democrat, pacifist, anti-war, feminist. I believe in the consensus process rather than Robert's Rules of Order, when practical. I would normally not be found hanging around with Darren in the next couple of lifetimes.

The love in the 12-Step fellowship does expand all those political and physical boundaries, so I can drive him to dinner and mean the love I feel for him in a legitimate fashion, yet in a platonic way, as a friend. In the 12-Step fellowship we share our raw, honest emotions with fellow members. We become good friends with people from all of society's diverse groups when sharing our most intimate thoughts, feelings, and actions about our personal recovery program. Even sharing in the general sense, over time people get close. I can be a left-wing activist, an anti-violence, pro-peace pacifist, and a die-hard liberal, and still love my fellow flag flying Republican man without wanting to marry him. I really want to stay sober and love everybody who shares this devastating disease together, one day at a time.

I do care if Darren lives or dies, but come on, this is not the relationship we have. I've been clear. I'm not sure how to continue, but I will not be driving him to dinner again or taking him to a meeting. He is being relentless, and I am now the naïve fool for thinking we both believed we were just friends.

Again, Darren asks me to think about his offer as he steps out of my car. I hate rejection more than anything in the world, but I need him to hear me. Once again, I say "No, I'm not interested in you in that way, I do not have to think about it".

I am left wondering if when I flip my hair or smile

a lot, my usual nervous gestures in public settings, am I sending the wrong message? Could it be perceived as flirting? When Darren and I walked into meetings together and sat next to one another, did people see us as a couple? Did Darren see us as a couple? Dang, is it just being female that set him up with these unrealistic expectations? I will no longer use my sexual energy as a woman in or around him. I'm not sure I really have, but I will forevermore pay attention to when, where, and how I give feminine messages or pheromones around the male species, especially Darren.

I ran into Darren a month later at a meeting. "Have you thought about my offer?", he asks. "You heard me before, the answer is no," I reply. Then, I started avoiding him and noticing our differences.

I must wonder if I am just too picky since a companion is what I long for. Is it too much to hold off for a spark, at least in the beginning? I am looking for someone that I'm drawn to, who is also attracted to me. I feel like there is a twenty-year age gap between us, but my reality is sometimes off. I remind myself that mutual love and adoration are possible. I don't regret this decision, and I do know love exists. I've experienced it, more than once. Then everything changes.

3 THE WILD YEARS - 1974

I just wanted to love and to be loved. From age fifteen to thirty, I am too young to give up on some sort of spark. To be adored, appreciated, and respected, that would be great too. I wanted to share my life with someone truly grateful for having found me, and someone I feel that exact feeling toward. It would set the stage for me to relax. To move into the next phase of my life in a partnership, with dignity and grace, and a sense of security too. I have wanted a partner for all these years. I have a journey that is not complete. I have hope that before I die, I will find love. I want mutual love, and it will have been worth the wait.

While in high school my first love was Joshua. He was unique and we shared an interest in Cat Stevens; the man and the musician. Joshua and I met on a spiritual level through the words and works of this amazing artist. Just as our love began to grow toward what I considered to be a lifelong path, I moved to Florida with my sisters. I was sixteen. While leaving the suburbs of Detroit and moving to the Sunshine State with my sisters seemed like a

Single and Sober: Who Found My Slipper?

delightful option, I found love and it also felt devastating to leave the man I wanted to spend my life with.

Our parents were late-stage alcoholics. My eighteen-year-old sister raised my middle sister and I from the time I was eleven and our middle sister was thirteen. The prior two years our parents were spiraling toward their bottom. We lost the house we grew up in and moved into the projects in Nor-Wayne, Michigan, twenty miles outside Detroit. These were temporary quadplexes built in WWII meant to be torn down afterward, still the slums of the neighborhood today. The area is called shack town. They were affordable, though. Our big sister was truly a hero and took care of my sister and I during those years and beyond, when our parents couldn't. She was just a teenager herself.

Custody became official two years later as our oldest sister became our legal guardian and our mom signed over custody through the courts so my sister and I could enroll in school. By then my sisters were twenty-one and fifteen, I was thirteen. I remember hearing the judge tell her, a twenty-one-year-old taking legal responsibility for two teenagers, she better not use public resources to support us. We were too proud to consider that an option, and too brow beaten by our father's pride to ever accept state assistance, but that judge was certainly no help.

Still, I was grateful I could legally enroll in school and felt a never-ending bond with my sisters from then on. Add my brothers then seventeen and sixteen, and we called ourselves a five-pointed star. Forever bonded in this world We were war zone buddies, the survivors.

It would be years later when I would question that judge who ordered my sister not to take help from a system set up to be a safety net for families like ours. My oldest sister worked two jobs. Our middle sister and I finished school while working part time paying the rent and other bills to make ends meet.

How our older sister had the wherewithal to step up to the plate without any role model, mentor, or much family support is beyond me to this day.

At eleven years old I was hitchhiking from Wayne to Ann Arbor, Michigan looking for boys and a party.

By sixteen, I had taken a break from doing most drugs. My big sister had that effect on me. I was crushing on my future life partner like most normal teenagers, but I had to follow my sisters to Sunny St. Pete and leave my soulmate behind. I was starting my senior year in high school when we moved to paradise.

After exchanging many love letters and cards with my boyfriend from Detroit, I received a card that said, "Someone else has claimed my love for you as their own". Dang. I was so certain we would someday build a life together. He met someone else, ended up marrying her, had a child, and took my heart with him.

I went on to date many men while I was looking for love. The artist, the Irishman, the father of my child. I've changed their names to protect the innocent. I began a quest to find my soulmate that would become quite an adventure. I always left one slipper behind just in case prince charming would find it.

I went on to find love as a youngster, a lot. I did not distinguish between lust, love, sex, a lover, and a friend. I did not care. I had passion and shared it. I had my morals, mind you. I used birth control and practiced safe sex. I never had more than one partner at a time. I never cheated.

Single and Sober: Who Found My Slipper?

I seriously tried to find my forever love.

Once I slept with a musician friend, a man that I loved, who never looked at me twice until the moment he came on to me out of convenience in the middle of the night. While I began to date someone else at that moment in time, it was the closest I came to overstepping my morals, what little morals I had left during my party days. Since I was not committed to the guy I had just started dating, and I truly adored the man I slept with, who naturally wanted nothing to do with me after he got what he desired, I did not consider that cheating. I had a lot of love and was not afraid to express it. Then, just before I got sober, I found Chase.

Prior to meeting Chase, I tried dating a few guys from my music days, my dart throwing times, and my bartending years. At first, I was attracted to the singers, song writers, and folk song lovers.

I was playing music at the local honkytonks and beach bars in Sunny St. Pete. For a decade I played guitar and sang folk songs from my 70's repertoire, throwing in an occasional original tune. I hung out at the taverns and beach bars around the Gulf of Mexico between Madeira and St. Petersburg Beaches where I resided at the time.

Eventually I acquired melanoma. Being an Irish sun worshiper who never could tan, it didn't stop me from trying. I ended up with the deadliest of all skin cancers, and moved to the Pacific Northwest known for the rainy and gloomy skies that could potentially keep me alive.

Once I went on a date with a local musician who took me to a tavern. He couldn't afford dinner but was willing to split a draft beer and a pre-packaged hoagie roll. I was cool with that. Some old drunk guy next to me at the bar reached up and pinched my boob. I wasn't cool with that. I slapped him. My date didn't notice.

I was developing feelings for an Irishman when I took a pre-planned vacation to MI. I got off the plane telling my sister I found the man I was going to marry. When I returned to FL he picked me up at the airport and informed me he got back with his ex while I was away. At least he was honest and let me spend the evening processing my feelings.

Later, I started joining dart teams and seemed to date the best darn dart players in the Tampa Bay area. Just when I liked someone, I'd find out they were no longer "broken up" with their exes, or they never broke up to begin with. Sometimes they would get back with their exes but neglect to inform me.

I had some exciting times with one of the dart champions of the region, Matt. I felt honored that he asked me to be his dart throwing partner at the Regional Soft Tip Dart Event in Orlando as it was highly competitive, and I was an amateur. Wasn't I surprised that he would be the one to freeze once we made it to the playoffs, and I would take home the win for us. I walked away feeling lucky to hold us up and to be seen with him. That only lasted until we got back in town, and I learned that he had not really broken up with the ex like he told me. Disappointing, but clearly Matt was not meant to be in my life longer than our out-of-town excursion where we had an exceptionally good time together.

Finally, I started bartending at one of the taverns where I used to play music. I was able to make more money and rely on a more reliable income, but I had to work double the hours and not have half the fun being a bartender versus the entertainment. It was nice not to have to "be on" all the time though.

I did have some sick fun at work one night. I recall being pursued by one of the cute regular customers, Devin, over months, right into the bedroom. The next night he brought in his wife who he was still with to play darts while I was bartending. I was mortified, as all the regulars knew of our affairs in this small community, and I had no clue he was married. I still had morals at this point in my drinking and using career. I waited until his wife was not present before reacting to him directly, although that was a difficult thing for me to do at the time. Patience was not my virtue. I bought Devin a free pitcher of beer and poured it over his head slowly right in front of the entire bar. Then I gave his wife a polite phone call so she would know who she'd married.

After all these false starts, it was a pleasure to meet my soulmate, the person who I'd been waiting for and who in the not-too-distant future would become the father of my baby, Chase. I had to move to the Pacific NW to follow my destiny; to become a drunk, a lover, and a mother first.

4 FLORIDA TO OREGON - 1989

Searching for myself and Prince Charming, I had to do another geographical move. After a decade in FL, it was 1986 when my oldest sister discovered she had melanoma. We used to lie in the sun. A lot. We were young, Irish women, always burning our skin. Often to the point of blistering. At best we would expose more freckles when the burns eventually subsided. Occasionally we ended up in the emergency room from severe sunburn and sun poisoning. Once the dermatologist diagnosed my sister with melanoma, she was taken in for immediate surgery. This involved skin grafting. She was told to never sunbathe again, always to wear sunscreen, and to have all of her immediate family members checked for melanoma.

I thought, "Well, you can't lay in the sun, but that doesn't mean I can't!" Two weeks later I was under the knife with the same surgeon. I had a 5 mm (about 0.2 in) spot of melanoma on my calf the size of a pencil eraser that required removing the skin around it to the bone, leaving a scar the size of a large bar of Ivory soap. Since I was a sun worshipper, if I wanted to live, I would need to go someplace where the sun rarely shined. I planned to move for a couple years then off to the Pacific Northwest I went.

I got off the plane saying I was not going to keep the Florida lifestyle of drinking and drugging up in Oregon. I would find myself a lumberjack to help me live in the mountains and be at peace with the beautiful scenery. I needed to stop living the insanity of the 80's, in beach bars, and with beach bums. I meant it. A fresh start was needed to save my life on so many levels.

Since I had been working at the dog track in St. Petersburg, FL, I pre-arranged a job at the dog track in Gresham, OR. I was hired sight unseen by a fancier restaurant than the cocktail lounge I had worked at in FL. I set up renting a couch with a friend and I flew the friendly skies.

The dog track job was a nightmare, but it allowed me to rent an apartment and buy a cheap car. I couldn't handle the outdoor restaurant stress of carrying heavy pewter plates up bleachers, so I quit as soon as I could find something better. Soon enough I was back to bartending, dating, and recreating my life across the country. Drugs, sex, and rock-n-roll.

5 CHASE - 1990

I was in love with Chase. I became crazy in love with my life partner, lover, drug dealer, bartender, and friend, Chaaaase. Our relationship was fueled by intensity, love, lust, passion, crazy fun and excitement. I needed to grow up, be a mom, and be there for our kid. Chase was not ready to clean up and be a dad until several years later. I was grateful for having known the passion, felt the love, survived the heartbreak, and (mostly) enjoyed the shared parenting of our child for the next twenty years.

Chase hooked up with a deeply religious, beautiful, chocolate skinned woman from Africa, quite progressive for this white small town country boy. They got married, had a bunch of kids, and he was a good dad to our son. He paid child support and took our son in when he longed for his daddy. I have no complaints about how our relationship and our son turned out. At that time, it felt more like a twenty-year relationship, but looking back we were only together for two passionate, crazy, drinking and drug-filled years.

We met at The Stagecoach Saloon twenty miles

Single and Sober: Who Found My Slipper?

outside Portland, Oregon. I was looking for a little cocaine because I had a girlfriend drive out from the city to visit and play darts. She was a master level steel dart player and I wanted to impress her. She shared drugs with me previously and I wanted to return the favor. It seemed that the only drug available in Gresham or Troutdale, Oregon was speed. Crank was not my drug of choice, it made me jittery, and I couldn't shoot darts well. I never really liked Meth, but it was given as a tip regularly and I got hooked on it anyway. Methamphetamines were everywhere in and around Gresham, Oregon.

I did it 'because it was there', but that specific night was special, and I wanted to get a better drug to share. It was such a delightful experience when I not only met Chase, but he shared his cocaine with both of us that night. He caught my attention and we immediately started hanging out.

At first our relationship was both edgy and sweet. He and I would drink and do drugs together and have intimate talks all throughout the night. He would be part of my crazy after-hours parties when The Stagecoach closed. Or I would go to the small-town tavern where he worked. The Springdale Tavern was a friendly place, and I would often hang out there until closing. Sometimes, after our bars closed, we would go to my apartment to sing and play guitars. Chase was living with his mother and her new husband and started staying overnight with me instead.

A few of our friends, regulars from The Stagecoach, would join us. Chase had a terrific voice. Once he was intoxicated and his inhibitions were lifted, we started to perform duets for our friends. There is nothing like connecting when singing, intimacy at its finest. The kind that sends shivers down your spine.

It was super difficult to end up pregnant after only knowing Chase for three months. I was using protection, but I found a hole in my diaphragm after learning I was six weeks along. I always knew that if I got pregnant, I would have the child. My belief is that all women have the right to choose, and my choice, if I ever encountered such a moment, would be to make it work.

Chase was not as certain, with good reason, given not knowing one another for very long and partying the entire time. He left me for a few days to think and check in with his brother and father before he made his decision. "Do you love her, son?" was his dad's question. I am guessing his older brother told him about the ungodly amount of child support he still owed his ex, and the financial burden it could pose should we not work out. I was set on having the baby. Chase finally said, "Yes, let's have this baby."

We both had a good time during the pregnancy at the taverns and with our friends. Tim, a lifelong friend and later my brother-n-law, was the "Pumpkin Prince of Mukilteo." He sat at The Stagecoach Saloon and carved a 200-pound pumpkin, which made the papers, while we sold raffle tickets as part of the baby fund. Neither of us had health insurance or any money in savings.

There were 50-50 baby pools at both bars guessing the day and weight of the baby. There were multiple baby showers, three in Oregon and one in Florida. We had everything we needed for the first two years, eventually getting temporary state insurance that covered the birth of our child. We had a lot of family and friends who offered emotional, material, and financial support.

I was shocked at how giving people were. It was the first time that I noticed the love from strangers as they showered us with homemade baby blankets and $100 tips. Even Chase's Dad gave us a $1,000 gift along with a three-foot teddy bear at our child's birth. I swore if I ever got my shit together and could give to strangers in need, I would buy gifts and make food like these people did that threw my parties.

I woke up early that rainy April morning in Boring, Oregon, overlooking the horse ranch located halfway up the mountain between Portland and Mount Hood. As I headed down the hallway of Chase's single wide mobile home, my water broke before I got to the bathroom. We had company that stayed the night before, Chase's brother, Mark, and one of his friends. The four of us were about to go out to breakfast. We didn't change our plans just because my water broke.

The Lamaze classes we took warned us about how long it can take to move labor along, so we weren't in a hurry to get forty minutes away to the hospital before the contractions had even started. I think back on that morning and wonder why having a baby didn't take priority over going out to breakfast with our hung over company. I couldn't eat, something unusual for me, as I was preoccupied with worrying about whether I would get to the hospital in time to deliver this baby. I recall breakfast taking forever and not having the voice to say, "we need to go."

I arrived at the hospital in time for the growing contractions, in time for having an epidural, and in time for our precious child to arrive safe and sound. He was the most unbelievable miracle in my life, and truly a gift from God. How he survived the party and baked in the oven coming out fully human without flaw is beyond me. He is blessed despite his mama and papa's troubled ways.

One of my favorite memories being with Chase was loudly singing Fleetwood Macs' "Landslide" on the Oregon Coast walking down the beach. We packed up our six-month old baby. We filled the cooler with beer, took a few baggies with crank or coke, I forget now, and headed to Chase's family cabin on the Pacific Ocean to conjure up a plan to stop using drugs. After taking a hike in the mountains, we walked along the sandy shore surrounded by picturesque rocks protruding out of the ocean. We had our hands around each other's backs and lifted our legs in time, swinging to the left, then stomping our weight to the right, while belting out, "I Took my love, I took it down / Climbed a mountain and I turned around / And I saw my reflection in the snow-covered hills, 'til the landslide brought me down /".

Chase was trying to teach me harmony to the bridge, which I could mimic when he sang, but out of habit I would take the lead whenever I was supposed to take over the harmony. I recall the intensity of being in the moment, being present, and being in tune with one another. Eventually, I held the harmony while he sang like a bird on the lead of the chorus, and wow, it was spectacular.

I do not recall where our son was at that moment, but we were having the perfect buzz, making a lasting memory, and feeling the love. The intensity of the music, the mountains, the coast, and the energy was magnified by the drugs. I knew beyond a shadow of a doubt we were meant for one another. We were growing as adults and we both desired to stop the hard drugs and start our life as parents together, as a couple in love. We had started a family.

We talked for days without much, if any, sleep. The drugs and euphoria made it impossible to slow down, let alone sleep. We invented the STOP program. We used all the drugs we brought over the weekend. When we were offered the white stuff, the plan we came up with was to STOP. **S**top. **T**ake control. Call each **O**ther. Have a **P**lan.

We headed home from that weekend having conquered our desire to continue our dependence on cocaine and crank. We would still drink beer, that wasn't a problem. We would smoke pot to help with the cravings. We would lick this thing that was taking over our lives. We had a plan to STOP the daily use of the white drugs for thirty-days. We were hopeful and motivated. And we were very high.

The next six months were a living hell. I was the first to run into that same dart master friend from Portland who offered me the white stuff. I was on day eleven of thirty. I got high, and before I headed home, I called Chase. I didn't have the language to say I had relapsed, just the story that "oops, I used the white stuff." Chase's response was classic: "That's okay honey, we won't count that." *Cool*, I thought, *this is my kind of plan*.

It was too scary to give drugs up completely at that time. I did continue through the thirty days, making it nineteen days consecutively off cocaine and meth, while continuing to drink alcohol and smoke pot. We started using meth again daily once we proved to ourselves it wasn't a problem. We could quit anytime we wanted. We truly did not think drinking and smoking weed was something we needed to stop.

Speed was available everywhere from so many people we knew. We created this environment. Chase stopped selling cocaine to become the best Dad he could be, which was very admirable, only we continued to snort crank. I never even liked it, but I found I could not live without it. *Just a little to get through the day,* I'd lie to myself. As soon as I'd start to come down, I'd have to do more, as the withdrawal was miserable. The next thing you know, I'd be up for days in a row, doing a drug I didn't even like, while trying to be the best mom I could be. It was insane.

I hated bringing a child into this world in a home that was filled with addiction. I had to use meth to function. I snorted so much my nose constantly bled. I could not get through a day without the drug I hated the most. It is a horrendous feeling of being controlled by a substance that you do not want to use and cannot stop from starting. *I'll quit tomorrow*, I kept telling myself, and I meant it. Every day became the same until I was done. I despised myself for bringing a child into this world when I was dependent upon being high, always wanting our child to sleep until noon. I sought out babysitters that only smoked pot or only drank, so he was not exposed to the hard stuff except at home. It was such a crazy time.

For four days we were on a binge without sleep or food, just snorting crank. Chase and I fought the entire time over getting clean or not. He wasn't ready and didn't think either of us had a problem. I noticed the similarities between our lifestyle and the home where I grew up. My folks were both alcoholics. My dad was controlling and probably mentally ill. Here we were fighting, arguing, in front of our baby. I was threatening to get clean. He was planning his suicide by driving off the Crown Point lookout on the Historic Columbia River Highway on the way to Multnomah Falls.

First, he wanted me to know it was my fault he was going to kill himself because I wasn't giving him the love he needed. He was depressed. Then, I was unhappy that I'd recreated my upbringing for another generation to attempt to survive. Geez, how did this happen? Finally, I was desperate and determined to stop this insanity.

I knew at that moment I was done using drugs, even if it meant I'd be a single mom, and I'd lose my soulmate, my best friend, and my drug using partner. I was ready to get help and desperate enough to make it a priority. I thank God every day for that moment of desperation in my life at that time.

I slept for the first time in four days and awoke to a phone call from my sister in Florida that our mother died. She and our father had been sober for about fifteen years by then. I knew in my heart of hearts that her baby (me!) was going to be okay, and she could leave this world now. My mother's spirit was cheering me on. I have felt divinely guided ever since, and my connection to God and my ancestors has grown from that moment forward. I know beyond a shadow of a doubt that my mother's spirit was making my life in recovery possible. I feel the presence of love surround me to this day, and I know that I am not alone in my recovery.

The following five months were torturous. Getting clean is not for wimps. I did not want to leave Chase. I wanted him to be ready to change his lifestyle with me. I stopped all mind-altering drugs and started attending intensive outpatient substance abuse treatment and self-help 12-Step groups. I began couples counseling with Chase. At the second session Chase told the counselor off and would not return after that. He was defensive and did not find that our lives needed changing. He was in denial, suicidal, and pretended everything was just fine. I have come to believe **FINE** stands for **f**–ked up, **i**nsecure, **n**eurotic, and **e**motional.

"You need to save that treatment slot for someone who needs it", Chase told me when I shared with him how excited I was to get into a free alcohol and drug treatment program.

My treatment counselor helped me brainstorm options of where to go when I left him and supported me in my toughest days of early recovery. How I stayed clean and sober in that house while he brought home the party every night, I will never know. All our friends were playing darts all night long, every night for the first five months of my sobriety. The darts were hitting the adjacent wall to my headboard while I was trying to get sleep. It really helped that I'd made up my mind that I was done using alcohol and other drugs. It also helped that I had loving spirits, (not the alcohol kind), guiding me back to sanity.

I found teenagers from a local church to babysit while I went to treatment. I paid for childcare so I could work a temporary job at a bank because Chase was too messed up to be awake in the daytime to take care of our son. I barely made enough money to cover the sitter, but it was important for me to be around productive mortgage brokers, all women who appeared to have their lives together.

Single and Sober: Who Found My Slipper?

I left for work when Chase was coming home from the after-hours party at the bar except on nights when the party was at our house. Later, I noticed Chase had punched a hole in the wall where my head would have been sleeping, after I moved out. I don't recommend starting your first five months of recovery in a drug-using home with all your friends hanging out while you plan your next steps toward finding a new way of life. I left in the nick of time; relapse was inevitable should I have stayed any longer. I was truly divinely guided.

I went to treatment and several types of 12-Step and other recovery meetings for support. I found a sponsor and went to meetings until I could live with the fact that Chase was not with me on this new path. I needed to leave him, or I would get high again. Chase's suicide plan became more focused as I began to change. I later learned that this is manipulation, not usually indicative of someone who wants to end their life, though homicide and suicide can be part of the package when control is threatened. Chase wanted me to go back to normal, and the threat of suicide was his way to get my attention. He got my attention all right, and it was the flame that fueled the spark for me to change the insanity of my life.

At first, my goal in going to meetings was to find a way to bring recovery home to Chase. I did not want him to die. I believed the lie that I would somehow be responsible for his choice to end his life. I only knew I could not keep up the lifestyle and raise our child while using drugs. I remember the war zone of both parents in their drunken stupors and the kids running the show. Chase and I were no better. I could not do that to our baby.

When our son turned one, I started my plan to move

out. I was five months clean and sober. I preferred to get an apartment nearby and co-parent with Chase, only I could not afford a place alone; my employment at the bank was temporary and it ended. I had no job and not much savings from the baby fund was left. I ruled out being homeless under the Burnside Bridge. I thought about moving in with my family to Michigan, Florida, or Washington.

I was in a bind and had to consider where I wanted to live for the next five years, according to my counselor. I picked Washington because it was close to my son's dad in Portland (a four-hour drive), and I could easily live with my oldest sister who had moved that summer from Florida to Washington to marry her childhood sweetheart. She brought along her two children, aged thirteen and eleven.

The newlyweds and adolescents welcomed my son and I with open arms, loads of love, and encouraged my healing time. It was one of the most precious times in my life. I sent out 150 resumes in those 3 months, and only got 3 interviews. I landed a job at 7-11 and sold beer for the following year, like a bartender but for a quarter of the pay. This and a few yard sales allowed me to get an apartment for my son and I.

I paid 50% of my wages for childcare and 50% of my earnings for rent. Our savings from the baby fund paid for phone, electricity, and gas. Eventually I learned to tap into the social service safety net programs. WIC, food stamps, and welfare (AFDC) compensated until child support was ordered by the court. It was humiliating to become a welfare mom for that temporary period of my life, but it was necessary to survive.

The biggest changes occurred at the end of my first

year of recovery when I found a sponsor in Washington and began to work the 12-Steps. I was fortunate to receive a housing voucher in my second year of recovery, as well as school grants, so I could switch to part time work and full-time college. Next to being a mom, college became my priority for the next eight years, until I could get a degree that would allow me to begin to earn a living wage.

At first, we had to live in the projects in Everett, WA, which had been newly renovated, and the units were nice. We had a view of the Cascade Mountain Range out the picture window from the living room. There were great neighbors all around us from different countries that introduced us to other languages, foods, and cultures. I did not want to leave there, but eventually we moved closer to where I attended college.

It was a miracle that after four years at Edmonds Community College and another four years at the University of Washington, I could begin to earn a living. Unfortunately, I had to intern in each of the programs I entered. First the addictions certificate program, then the BA social welfare program, and lastly, the master's program for Social Work. I was annoyed by all the "free labor" expected to be given in those five years of interning, but grateful my trainee position allowed for some paid internships while I gained knowledge and competence in working with people addicted to substances.

I met many people during those eight years of college, but rarely dated until I was in my last couple of years. I was too busy being a single mom, getting my son off to school, and coordinating childcare before and sometimes after school. I would try to get to recovery meetings to stay sober and work with my sponsor and sponsees, never quite feeling like I was doing enough. All the while, I worked and/or interned in the human service field, intentionally writing my resume so when I graduated, I could enter my career with some job experience.

Those eight years went by quickly, but they were grueling. The first two years Chase fought the child support process until the state got involved and started garnishing his wages. Luckily, he didn't go underground like his brother and so many others did to avoid paying toward their children's care. He went from selling drugs to selling cars and without the constraints of having a family he went into a larger tax bracket while I went into poverty.

In college I learned how normal that scenario is for families that separate, and it was a light bulb moment for me. It drove my desire to work with, and for, women in poverty as a career focus. Eventually, I became a women's advocate working with survivors of domestic violence. I used my training and experience in recovery from substance abuse to develop programs that reached the heart of the intersection between safety and sobriety. If I had not known who the father of my baby was, if he had gone underground, or if the safety net in the system had failed me, I would not have been able to escape poverty.

I have come to notice how being a poor white woman with only one child has placed me in a privileged position. The odds of escaping poverty became almost insurmountable for me but would have been so much worse if I were a black woman, an immigrant, or a black or brown woman with multiple children.

My teachers, professors, and bosses have mostly

spoken my language, had my skin color, and "judged me" based on their limited norms. The closer I look like them in race and age, the more I speak like them in verbiage and slang, and the more I act like them in pretending I'm a normie without emotional baggage, the better my chances of gaining and maintaining an education, employment, and advancement.

It helped that in higher education my teachers looked like me; they were mostly white and from the city or suburbs. It did not hurt that I was prepped with a grade school education that taught me from this Century's classroom books, and my professors graded me accordingly. I acknowledge I have been privileged to change my tax bracket, and it is not equal access for all. Pulling oneself up by the bootstraps is a lie.

Years later, I would become the Manager of the local Crisis Line and work in Suicide Prevention. It worked out well that lived experience became popular about the time I quit caring if my bosses, colleagues, and clients knew I was in recovery. I was taught to silence that fact during most of my career, as it could have negative consequences. That was smart advice. Not only did it put my non-recovering colleagues at a disadvantage, but I have also had my clients use it against me by breaking my anonymity telling others they saw me at a meeting. I once had a client tell my boss what she shared at a meeting and had expected my boss to have this information because I was at that meeting, too. Anonymity is hard to pronounce and even harder to abide by its intent. I get to decide if anyone knows I'm in recovery. When we are anonymous, the I is set aside. We can do together what we couldn't do alone.

My colleagues and others judged me harshly. I had taken on the persona of my clients, regardless of how many decades I was clean and sober. I always reminded someone of their relatives' nasty behavior, so they disliked me before knowing me. It wasn't until I became more comfortable in my own skin that I quit caring what others thought of me, it is none of my business.

Once I was able to become licensed as a therapist, I was able to add Mental Health into the mix of areas where I had at least some expertise. I had to take the Social Work licensing exam three times, despite testing toward the end of my career. Maybe I burnt out too many brain cells using alcohol and other drugs, perhaps I have test anxiety, or maybe the Licensed Clinical Social Worker test is geared for only a select few to pass. I was considered a specialist by then, which also interferes with passing this generalist's test.

Intellects that can use five-point logic and read between the lines to find the correct answers on the exam were the only ones to pass that new exam in the late 90s and early 2000s. I kept trying until the twenty-fifth year of my career when I could finally pass the exam that would allow me to make a living wage working only one job.

Eventually, I would specialize in working at the intersection between intimate partner violence, substance abuse, and mental health. Any door, similar problems. Housing and homelessness go hand in hand, too. This is my work, my life, my passion. Personal? Yes, every Step of the way.

It took a long time to get past Chase. For eight years I focused on school. I kept my head down. Toward the end of my college years, it was time to reconsider adding love to my life, again. Open to love and available, I made a commitment to myself to look up.

6 LOOKING UP - 2000

I loved before I met Chase and knew I would have intimacy like that again. A few years after Chase and I split up, I was ready to date again. I felt the pain, grieved the loss, and knew more about myself and the type of guy I was looking for.

However, I was reluctant to put a stepdad into my son's life, so I was not in a hurry. All my friends that were also single moms were hooking up with boyfriends, having them move in, and they had their kids call them "dad". Then six months later the latest dad would be gone. Before the year was out there would be another man, a new dad. Repeat the scenario. No, I was not going to do that to my son.

I kept my head down, went to college, worked, and raised my boy. I went to the next college, interned, studied, graduated, and did it all again in even higher Education. For my master's in social work graduation, I bought a house as a graduation present, moved to the suburbs, and continued to make it a point to "look up". My son was in the sixth grade. We were ready. "Ok, God, bring it on",

Single and Sober: Who Found My Slipper?
was my mantra. I'm ready to find love now.

MatchMaker.com, Match.com, Speed Dating, SpeedDating.com, OurTime, Events and Adventures, Singles Meetup Groups, Love/Match.com, eHarmony, more speed dating and eventually the pathetic, PlentyOfFish.com. Plenty Of Fish is a free site that attracts the sickest of people.

Many, many, many stories. Many dates. Much laughter. The ads are ridiculous, the muscle shirts and motorcycles, the men who want to attract men with their sports and fishing brags, and the pictures that are a decade or two old. Meeting men that look like the father of the person you are expecting to meet is an odd experience. It's such a weird time. Bars were so much simpler.

Only that's not who I am now. My judgment was impaired when I was intoxicated. Without my inhibitions lifted, it's more difficult for me to let someone know when I am interested. Unless it's a perfect match, someone always gets rejected. I have more fear around being hurt and/or hurting others to continue with online dating for more than a month or so before I need to take a break for a while. Still, I have a desire to have that perfect match, so I go for the odds. Eventually, I must meet my match, right?!?

7 TOM – SPRING 2002

I am excited to meet Tom. He shows up to our coffee date in a yellow work van, acting embarrassed for me to notice. The yellow was the fluorescent kind, deep yellow like mustard, but brighter, much brighter than the sun. However, it didn't bother me. I really don't care what he drives unless it's totally a tweaker mobile. He explains that he collects antique cars and couldn't get his favorite one running tonight. No problem, that's not important to me. We connect. He wants to take me out for dinner next time, that's cool. Supper is good. I love food. Hard to get to know someone over a one-hour coffee date, but it can rule out the 'beyond a doubt not a match' group.

Tom pre-plans the adventure. He takes me up north an hour away to a special restaurant. Tom shows up in a late model sedan, sweet. New and clean, he went to some trouble. He says he rented it. What? Now that is going the extra mile, for sure. Pun intended. He didn't want to take me out in his bright yellow work van or break down in his antique car, so he rented a car for our first real date, and he did make it special. Ahhh. I'm impressed. The

Single and Sober: Who Found My Slipper?

restaurant pick in Antecortes was delightful and delicious, overlooking Fidalgo Bay and the San Juan Islands. He took me on a short, lovely hike nearby on the water and that added a perfect sunset ending to a well thought out and relaxing date. Very cool. Let's do it again, oh hurry quick. I like this man.

I have a three-date rule that I'm not going to let myself be too vulnerable with someone I meet online. I always meet in a public place until at least the third date and I get a better sense of who they are.

Tom wants to show me his cabin on the river in the mountains. He can't stop talking about it. Oh my, how great that sounds. I know the area. It's one of my favorite spots on earth. He wants to show me his antique car collection, too. *Sure.* Antique cars are not my thing, but clearly, they are what he's interested in. *That would be fun,* I say to myself. Is this a third date since we met for coffee initially, or is it a second date? Should I go to the mountains with this nice man, alone? *He doesn't look like a mass murderer. I don't think someone looking to kill you would rent a car to take you to dinner.* He brought me back to our meeting place. A respectful peck on the cheek. Sweet. Sure, I'm going to see his cabin in the mountains on the river. You betcha. Second date or third date, it doesn't matter. He's a nice guy, cute, thoughtful, and very sweet.

We met for lunch first. *Oh my, your hands are greasy,* are my thoughts. Tom apologizes as he had to put his seat in the car this morning so I could ride with him. We planned to ride in his antique vehicle from the last small town where we met for lunch, Monroe, before heading into the Cascade Mountains. His cabin is in Index located in front of the North Fork of the Skykomish River overlooking Mount Index.

We went out to the parking lot to find his antique car and I got in. *How nice of him to put in the seat this morning, he really went all out, again. Well, gosh, where is the dashboard? Oh look, the floor is nothing but rust. There is no upholstery. This is such a piece of junk, but at least it runs. Well, I'm hoping it does.* I do not want to get stranded in the mountains because his car won't make it up or down the hill. I'm hoping the rest of the collection is cute, and the cars run, but I'm not convinced that will be the case.

After he bought my second meal, I feel obligated to continue our date as planned, though I'm feeling skeptical. I ignored my intuition about this adventure and left with him anyway. Tom is excited to show me his cabin, and I'm willing, but wondering if it's the best choice to leave my vehicle behind.

The feeling of shoving my logical and wiser self under the rug reminds me of when I was a young woman. My dates would expect something in return for their "putting out" (i.e., paying for dinner or a meal), so I did. In this case, I knew I was not expected to "put out", but I did feel obliged to go see his cabin and to drive in his antique junk mobile to get there, despite my intuition telling me otherwise.

We headed up the mountain highway and eventually arrived safely at his cabin. There is a double wide pole barn made of metal that hovers over about fifty pieces of what looks like scrap metal. Evidentially, this is antique scrap metal. There are frames without bodies, no engines in any of them, no exteriors, no interiors, just simply piles and piles of junk metal. I think they are cars. Wow. This is so sad. "Tom, how long have you been collecting these?" I ask. "Thirty years", he replies.

Oh, this is pitiful. He has yet to restore even one. I think the first attempt was today, putting in a seat in the only car with a frame. I'm guessing he had to put in the engine, too. Dang, what a hobby.

I am anxious, nervous to go next door to see inside his river cabin he talks so much about. We strolled fifty feet to a cute little cabin overlooking the river. Both the river and the cabin are simply beautiful.

Walking in, I nearly fell through the floor, caught only by the subflooring. It turns out the cabin had flooded years ago. The floor had rotted out and there were water marks visible about four feet off the ground throughout the cabin. The stench of mold is overwhelming, but I managed to make my way through to the back of his one-bedroom oasis so he could show me the pictures of the UFOs on his wall. Tom becomes animated when talking about the government's conspiracy to restrict people who have spotted UFOs from talking to one another. He talks about electromagnetics and antennas, and I suddenly say my lunch is not settling well and I need a ride back to my car. Tom obliges and I leave that mountain and never look back.

8 TIM – SPRING 2003

In the beginning of online dating, I would stay on the dating site for weeks before giving out my email, then spend weeks emailing back and forth, and slowly, if I still felt there could be a fit, I would give out my phone number. This is how it went with Tim.

What I loved about Tim is that he was right in my neighborhood. In fact, we probably walked our dogs past one another. He lived in the apartments on the corner of my street about five blocks away and said he was living with his daughter helping her out with rent.

When I later looked back on it, what I didn't like about Tim was that we talked about so many things before we ever met. We discussed past relationships, children, jobs, friends, and I felt like I really knew him. I was overly invested in our bond before I even set eyes on him. We shared things that were not appropriate for strangers to know about one another, all in the desire to trust and be vulnerable seeking love.

I was surprised when I finally met him for dinner, and I thought I was meeting the father of the person I had been talking to. *Are you kidding?* Tim is clearly twenty years older than his MatchMaker.com picture. It becomes apparent during our first live conversation that he can't keep a job; he lives off his daughter, and therefore, he is not a person of character. He lies, or at minimum is deceitful. Tim's work ethic makes him unemployable, and what man of integrity relies on his daughter to support him?

I am thankful for Tim because he taught me that regardless of my perceived screening and weeding out the crazy ones and those eager beavers, that I can still be fooled. There are people who participate in online dating who are dishonest, lying behind the safety of the computer screen. Thank goodness he wasn't dangerous, that I saw him for who he was in person, just not who he said he was via email. I never saw Tim again. I let him buy me dinner and I spoke my truth behind the safety of my computer screen; uh no, not interested.

9 PICK ME - 2004

I really put myself out there for the next seven years. Every chance I had to meet someone for coffee, to attend a speed dating event, or to socialize at a single's mixer, I was there. Knowing that I can make a positive first impression and I am able to be social, I found the speed dating events to be fun. Eventually, one must make a match.

I increased the odds by deciding to 'pick' at least half of the men I met as a choice for a second date. That was usually about five or six men per event. After ten six-minute dates I knew enough to rule out five, but not enough to know if any of the other five could work. It's all about the odds. If any of them picked me, then we could have a second date.

I was dumbfounded when no one ever picked me. What the heck? There were two basic themes for these occasions that included my age group: one was active, and the other was business. Since I'm both, I figured I could fit into either. I was surprised to find the active group were people who climbed Mount Rainier or bicycled from Seattle to Portland, ha, no not really me. The business folks were conservatives that wanted to know my fiscal beliefs in the beginning of our six-minute date, which was weird. Still, I found there to be a half dozen I would date again from both groups, over and over at these events. Nobody ever picked me, which I simply could not understand, as I felt prepared, charming, lighthearted, but not a dingbat, and fun-loving. Do people really make connections at these events? I was beginning to have my doubts.

10 KENNY – MARCH 2006

Kenny came along and gave me hope. It was great. I finally got picked at a speed dating event. I knew we made a connection, though I was beginning to doubt my own reality. He was also a social worker, totally focused on being in the moment and had some sweet and thoughtful questions for me.

How would I describe my favorite dessert? How cool, a fun "get to know you" question. When I learned he was blind, it made good sense, too. How does one notice and describe what they see to a blind person? I could see myself with him, pardon the pun. He was a bit younger than me, but we totally connected in ways that were hard to describe. I did not know at that moment that he would pick me, and when I learned this, I was thrilled.

It was unfortunate that I got home from the event to learn he picked me, and I knew that I was leaving to go camping in the mountains for a week the next day. I sent him an email to let him know I was excited that we picked each other, and I looked forward to seeing him again. Also, I let him know that I would not be in cell range for reception of emails or phone calls for the next week.

It didn't matter. He never contacted me again. Was it that I was too old? Too whatever, fill in the blank. Clearly that was not meant to be. Maybe he picked five women, too. For whatever unknown reason I was picked by one man, a blind man, who ghosted me. My confidence started to wane. It gave a whole new meaning to a blind date.

11 ROSS – DECEMBER 2007

I hadn't seen Ross in nearly fifteen years when I ran into him again. I was so crazy about Ross back in 1993 when we shared the same home group. He looked like the once famous Marlboro Man from cigarette commercials back in the day. Sexy, thin, artist, rugged cowboy type; I used to get so nervous to talk to him. We shared our first years in recovery together, hanging out, playing guitars. Skinny dipping'. Well, I kept my clothes on while Ross and his friend, Deano, skinny dipped.

Ross used to talk to me for hours about the nudist lifestyle he led. I was so naked-phobic it intrigued me to think about someone who lived in a nudist camp who swears that it's not about sex, it's about judging a person by their character. *Really?* How cool to buck the system and throw away your Anne Kline and Eddie Bauer to equal out the playing field. Doctors are now equal to street bums, nobody's got on clothes, and all is well in the world. Ha-ha. I had no interest in becoming a nudist, since I could barely walk around alone at home without clothes on. But I was extremely interested in Ross.

He was the coolest man in the fellowship, a pretty

boy, radically different, and a musician. Yes Siree bob. Fire. I had the hots for Ross. It has always felt mutual. Somehow, we were led back together after years since he ran off to the nudist park with that girl from our home group. Now they've split up and he is single and lonely, too. Certainly, this is a sign from the powers that be. We start playing and hanging out 'til wee hours every night. The conversation is so natural. The electricity is clear, but he's not coming on to me. That's okay. We are bonding and it's so nice to not be pushed.

I must resist touching him all over. *Let him take the lead,* I remind myself. I can't seem to grow out of this lesson I was taught as a young girl. We are close. I want to see where our relationship goes, how it grows. I love getting to know him, earning the bond, learning his interests, and sharing our music. A natural fit, for sure. He's so tan. OMG, hot. Sizzling. I can't think straight.

We invited our recovery friends to join us; we started music night at my house. Ahhh, just like the old days. My life in sobriety is mimicking the intense fun from my days of using alcohol and drugs, but we are all sober. Everyone is laughing and singing in my living room. We're having a blast.

He offers to paint my house if he can do it in the buff. Well, sure. If I don't have to be nude, it's all good. We have a clothing optional painting party and invite some of our friends from the fellowship. It's just like the old days in early recovery when he held a clothing optional 12-Step meeting at the nudist camp. All the guys showed up and peeled off their clothes, all the women stayed fully dressed. Same thing with our painting party. Only two other people showed up to paint, another guy in the nude and my sponsor who also kept her clothes on.

Only after the other guy left did my sponsor and I let Ross use us as a vessel for his art project. He painted our body parts and rolled it out on butcher block paper. It was not sexual, but it was sensual and indeed fun. There was something so wrong about doing this with my sponsor, and something so natural about doing it at all. It didn't feel dirty or too weird, just fun and kind of like art. Silly art. Memorable art.

After the first couple months I started to get clarity of mind around Ross. I began to see that he had some interesting traits. First, he quit his job after a month because he could earn more money, but then he never went to work anywhere else or worked for himself like he planned. Ross also had some rather feminine qualities and enjoyed when he did dress, to dress like a woman. Not so much that it was blatant like wearing a dress, except on Halloween which he really enjoyed, and carried around pictures from those events, it was more subtle.

He liked truly short pink shorts so his penis would hang out. Those pink shorts did show off his nudist tan, but the private parts needed to stay private, in my opinion. Ross, it turns out, had some Narcissistic qualities that I had overlooked during my infatuation phase. He truly only thought about himself.

Then there were those depressed moods. It was hard to be around him when he was in his devastatingly sad times. He spewed negative energy that sucked those around him dry. I was scared he would kill himself when he was alone because at times, he was so focused on life not being worth living. It was awlful to watch him spiral down when the rest of our clean and sober crowd were so grateful and happy to be recovering our authentic selves from the horrors of our past.

It was taking the time to get to know him that I could get past the lust stage, come to my senses, and see Ross for who he was. I eventually became most grateful for the fact that I didn't become his girlfriend. I still thank the Universe for giving me time to figure out that Ross was infatuated with himself, incapable of making a living, unable to come out of his dark cloud, and most likely a depressed, anti-social, narcissist. How I nearly fell for a guy who couldn't keep his clothes on is freakin' beyond me. God is so good and does for me what I can't do for myself. Thank-you, thank-you, thank-you. I consider myself blessed. Amen.

12 ANDY – JUNE 2009

SpeedDate.com brought even more interesting dating experiences. In the half dozen times I drove to downtown Seattle and had ten six-minute dates in an hour, I thought for sure I would find someone where there would be a mutual spark. I am outgoing and my extrovert personality is sometimes enhanced by large quantities of caffeine. I figure it is a numbers game. I only need to rule out a few people each night that I don't want to see again. I was hoping to find five people I could get to know better and one that stood out.

I don't sense people are not attracted to me. I don't believe I am repulsive. Most of the time I feel like the girl next door. Not the model beautiful kind, not the homely sort, just an average woman next door. I make the effort to dress nicely and make myself presentable, even for coffee dates. Who knows why I don't get picked at these events, but the whole speed dating experience has left me feeling less than desirable and desiring to date less. I suppose I'm a diehard because I go away and then I always come back, as if I'm a masochist who can't get enough punishment.

Ever.

In addition to the speed dating events, there is also an online dating site attached to SpeedDate.com. I was approached by someone named Andy through the dating site who asked me to meet him for coffee. Ten years ago, I would wait forever to meet someone, but I now lean toward the other end of the spectrum. I'd rather meet someone rather quickly, see if there is a connection, and have a clue who I am communicating with.

Andy and I met at a coffee house in Everett near my work. As we chatted, we both saw potential in the possibility of a relationship. We have a few things in common: we enjoy health, nature, and we are hard-working people. I wasn't crazy about him, but he seemed to be nice enough and I wanted to see if we could build something starting with having similar interests. We decided to go for a hike near the beach on our second date and it was super sweet. We didn't plan the hike well because it ended abruptly after a quarter mile. This was a disappointment since we had trail mix and water, hiking clothes, and time for an all-morning workout. As it turned out, we were able to sit and talk, and that was great, too. We learned a bit about one another, and before we parted, we both agreed we'd like to see one another again. I am serious and not just placating him for fear of telling the truth.

Then the oddest thing happened. Andy emailed me a questionnaire. He must have found it in Psychology Today and I'm guessing it was meant for people considering marriage. There were lots of personal questions: where you prioritize money, expectations of your partner, how often you like sex, whether you want children, etc. I thought the questionnaire was insane, having had two dates, but I wasn't going to rule out the relationship because his sense of timing was off, like maybe two years premature.

I inquired if he was asking me to fill this out and send it back, or if he'd like me to sit with him and answer these questions. I also asked him if he would also be answering them and let him know my preference would be to sit together and answer them.

Wasn't I surprised to find how not only did Andy want me to fill out the questionnaire solo, but he was also unwilling to answer the same questions in return. *What?* He became pompous and needed me to answer these questions before deciding to continue 'investing' in me. So far, he shared his trail mix and a couple of hours, he had not invested much effort at all, and he isn't invested in sharing himself. He is only interested in judging me and withholding this personal information about himself. There is nothing mutual about this and it's weird. I am no longer interested in building a future with Andy.

I was not impressed when he was at the next speed dating event I attended. He didn't seem to remember me, and that is one guy I refused to pick in my 50% "I'd like to see again" responses at the end of that speed dating event.

13 DASHA – SEPTEMBER 2009

It was the mid-eighties when I first met Dasha back when I lived in Florida. What a cutie. An ex-Hari Krishna from the 70's, he kept the name. He continued to wear cotton, eat vegetarian, and love God, but he didn't shave his head or solicit money from the airport anymore. I connected with him through our shared love of music. He liked playing congas to my music, I liked doing cocaine with him and singing REO Speedwagon, "Heard it from a friend who / heard it from a friend, who / heard it from another you been messing around", high and drunk, laughing, and uninhibited. We had a super romantic fling.

Although I was still attracted, I broke up with him. We would get stoned, and I remember not trusting that he wouldn't fall asleep with a cigarette in his hand. It made me too anxious to fall asleep with him in my waterbed. I moved on. He did, too.

It wasn't long after that when he was visiting my house in Florida, my sister came down from Michigan to visit me. She was at the tail end of her first marriage, pregnant with her last child, and ready to move on from her marriage. She and Dasha clicked. They began a long-distance emotional relationship until my sister's husband moved out. Dasha and my sister then started a long-distance romance.

I do remember my sister and Dasha's relationship was intense for a year or so and their breakup seemed to involve threats of violence. Though, my sister disagrees with what I recalled about their time together. I'd heard he'd had a bad breakup with one of my friends just after we split up. With his relationship with my sister, as I remember, our dad was involved. There was some kind of scene at the airport; ugly, scary, somebody threatened to hurt someone. My sister thinks this memory pertained to someone else, but I remember something not right about him when ending it with both my friend and my sister.

Still, over the years I vacationed in Florida, often during a time when Dasha was around. We always flirted and continued to be attracted to one another. I moved to Portland, OR and later to Seattle. He moved to Boston. We still respected one another. But I got clean and sober and became active in the recovery community, and he kept using. He was smoking marijuana daily and drinking a little. We had different lifestyles for certain.

In 2009 he found me on Facebook, and we reconnected. I let him know I was recording an album of all original music and he said he was doing studio production work. That was cool. I needed someone musical to bounce things off, the production end was new and exciting, but I wanted more feedback than my limited musical friends in Seattle could offer. I started sending Dasha songs to critique and I simply loved his input. We were excited to work with one another on this project. In fact, he decided to fly out for my CD release party. How cool! I knew I was not going to be drawn in by his charm as he is a pot smoker, doesn't ever work a "real job," and I was concerned about how he exited his relationships in the past.

My sister was planning to come to Seattle for my fiftieth birthday party and the CD release party in the same week. It could have been awkward, so I was sure to check with her prior to letting Dasha buy a ticket. She was fine with the idea of him being here in the crowd staying at my house, it was over twenty years since she'd seen him last. She was now ending her second marriage after ten years and in a totally different emotional place. My sister said she held no regrets about Dasha, and she didn't recollect any violence or scary ending when they split up. Strange. I swear there was something ugly, maybe even dangerous.

I was excited to reconnect with him, especially around my music, and he was just as thrilled to be part of the big day. He offered to run sound at the carefully picked venue. It was held at an old church turned into a musician's haven called the Tim Noah Thumbnail Theatre in Snohomish, WA. I had a friend and music buddy scheduled to run sound who was also going to be playing and singing on a few tunes during my live CD release party. I knew Dasha's expertise would be welcomed and he was needed to sit in on sound. It would have been impossible for my friend to run sound and accompany me live simultaneously.

Dasha booked a two-week vacation, which I didn't really expect. My siblings all flew in, too, from FL and MI, that week. It was like my moment of fame. I could compare it to having a wedding since until this point in my life I had never had one. Turning fifty years old and putting out an album of all original tunes was so exciting. At times it was stressful and within days of one another it became overwhelming, but I wanted family to attend both events.

I had finally found my niche in writing about my spiritual healing journey and half the songs on my "Moments of Clarity" album were about this. I invited many of my friends to the recording studio to play or sing on my CD the year prior.

While my family all booked a one-week vacation for my two parties, the second week Dasha would be here by himself. I took extra time off work and planned to unwind and show him around some of the spectacular scenic spots in the Pacific Northwest while he was here.

The first week was a blur and so much fun. My oldest sister who lived nearby acted like I was getting married. For my birthday party she booked The Little Red Barn for the venue, run by the city of Marysville. That sister attempted to rent cloth linens and silverware, but I interrupted that process. It wasn't my wedding, and we were to gather at a Barn. "No linens or silverware allowed" says the birthday girl.

I invited everyone I knew to both events, but people only came as a crowd to the CD release party. The 50th birthday party at the Little Red Barn had a lousy turnout, but my family and a few special friends made it memorable. Dasha made East Indian food, everyone brought potluck items, it was sort of lame in that it was tiny, though it was intimately sweet, too.

The CD release party was my moment to shine, and I loved it. I was extremely hot due to the spotlight being too close to the stage, but I was able to play every song on the CD. I even gave an encore with the song I wrote for my son that wasn't finished in time for the album. It was raw, real, and unrehearsed. That song was too new to play on stage, but it worked okay for the occasion. I sang my heart out, got back-up from my friend on vocals and guitar on a few tunes, her husband played bass on a couple songs, and I was accompanied by Dasha on flute for one tune. What a fun night! I sold a lot of CD's, shared the proceeds with those who contributed musically, and still made a profit after paying for the rented space.

The entire week was electric. Dasha flirted the whole time, and I flirted back, all in fun. It wasn't until he explained he had two weeks off weed that I started to see him in a different light.

Huh. He asked me to take him to recovery meetings.

After my family left, I can feel my desire to go for it, but I'm also resistant because he works as a day trader in the stock market. He also lives in Boston, and I'm unsure if I want to get involved with him simply because of physical attraction. I decided to wait and see how the following week unfolded.

I took Dasha to my favorite places in WA. Up the Mountain Loop Highway one day and to Mount Baker the next. We explored the Skykomish River, Mukilteo Beach and took the ferry over to Langley to check out Whidbey Island and Deception Pass. Eventually we made it over Steven's pass to the German town.

He surprises me with a kiss in Leavenworth that brought me to my knees. The teens next to us asked us to get a room. Okay, that was fun. However, I stopped him. I am not ready to commit to being with him. I know we only have a week together and I make it clear I do not want a relationship with him long term. I tell him I am not committing to anything longer than this week. He says he's fine with that. I let myself have a fling for a week with an old flame. The electricity between us is undeniable. Plus, he's a good lover.

There were two significant things that did not feel right about Dasha. First, he had two weeks clean. When we talked on the phone about my recovery, he said he was attracted to it and decided to stop smoking marijuana. He wanted to go to recovery meetings with me. I took him to meetings, where he fit right in, but he was a newcomer.

In the 12-Step fellowships it is well known that you leave the newcomers alone. When you don't you are called a "13th Stepper". When someone with time in sobriety comes along and scouts out a newbie to have sex with, it often doesn't last. The person who has more time is usually better equipped to deal with a breakup than the newcomer who is more likely to relapse. "13th Stepping" is really frowned upon. I am the first to judge people for doing it. Pun intended.

In this scenario, I was screwing a newcomer, so wrong. I hate 13th Steppers. I kept trying to justify we were ex-lovers, but we were at different places in our journey and if it didn't work out, I could be setting him up for a relapse.

The other thing that I didn't feel right about was that he was crazy about me, and I did not feel the same way back. I liked him, I was having great fun, but he's about obsessing on the stock market and making pennies or dollars every day, sometimes hundreds of dollars up or hundreds of dollars down. That's gambling. Currently, I'd prefer to save for retirement and have a job that provides a regular paycheck to cover my mortgage and bills.

I don't want to take care of Dasha, I want someone who can pull their own weight. I am willing to have fun and play with him, but I'm not sure having a future with him is something I desire. With my broken brain, I can't afford to learn about day trading either.

I proceed with caution. The hours spent in the car traveling around to my favorite destinations were great. The Leavenworth kiss, spectacular. The romantic nights and mornings were super fun. Sneaking around so my son didn't know we were sleeping together was silly and weird. I knew if I could not tell my adult son and could not tell my home group, it probably wasn't right.

We went out to dinner with The Marlboro Man, Ross, and his new girlfriend. We had a nice double date, but again, I felt guilty for being with a newcomer. He needed to recover, not to start a relationship with someone with eighteen years of sobriety. At times I felt like a sponsor, not a girlfriend.

Then came the last night he was in town. Despite all the indecision, I began to wonder if we could work something out and start a long-distance relationship. Dasha became obsessed with helping me with home improvement before he left, and he decided to hang my new door that didn't fit my doorway. I told him not to bother, let's have a nice last supper, and I cooked a nice vegetarian meal with mushroom risotto, coconut curry, roasted vegetables, and a side of lentil soup.

Unfortunately, he didn't listen and proceeded to take on the hang the door project. He got half-way through and didn't have the tools he needed. Dinner was getting cold, so I asked him to take a break and eat, but he refused.

Instead, he went to the neighbors that had attended the birthday party to borrow tools and the next thing I knew, my neighbor was here taking over. Sure, my neighbor is good at this kind of work, but this was not how I wanted to spend our last evening together and I didn't care about the door.

Four hours later Dasha needs to pack and they're still at it. I decided to warm up dinner and eat alone, getting more and more pissed that he won't call it a night. Now the door is hung, but there is a two-inch gap at the bottom, and they start to clean up. I go to bed alone because it's the middle of the night and I don't care if they clean up or not. I don't like that the door now has an opening that will leave me cold all winter. Dasha is going to miss his plane if he doesn't get packed and get some sleep and I am disappointed not to get a relaxing and romantic dinner before his sendoff.

I drove Dasha to the airport the next morning and we agreed to stay in touch. I am going to give it a try, see how his recovery goes, and slowly talk about future potential. I really like the guy. I could grow to love him. I am certainly attracted to him, but I'm not 100% in. Again, we talked, and I agreed to proceed with caution.

The following two weeks were tough. He wants to talk every night for hours and hours and I'm just not into it. I want to watch The Biggest Loser on TV, to go to meetings, and to talk briefly. He wants to ponder how to change the world, how to reconnect, how to merge our lives. After about fourteen days I can't do it anymore. I let him know I want to back off. Naturally, I want to remain friends, I just need to bow out of the romance.

Then he upped the ante. Now he becomes suicidal

and needs to talk it out. Really? I sit with him on the phone for hours. I'm the friend that is going to walk through this with him. He gets through the moment. I sleep and wake up deciding that I'm done. I cannot go on seeing Dasha. I feel like I'm working on my off time.

I tell him, "Don't call me, I'll call you. I need a break". He calls and emails daily. Oh no, he won't let me back off or break up. I ignore him. He starts leaving me voicemails that he's sending me something expensive in the mail. I ignore him.

He sends me packages. I returned them to sender. He leaves messages about why I didn't say thank you for the gifts. I do not respond.

He sends more packages. I threw them away. He calls my brother, his friend, to get him to talk me into seeing him again. I sound like a lunatic to my brother responding to a simple message to call Dasha. "But", I say with such heightened energy, as if I'm the one who's off the hook, "he's crazy…", and I rant about it long enough for my brother to believe I am indeed the one with issues. Dasha drives from Boston to Tampa and talks to our mutual friends. They started to contact me to inquire why I wouldn't give him another chance.

This is the type of guy I've learned about after decades of working in domestic violence. When you can't take a break, and you can never break up, it's a sign of possession, of ownership, and it is not good. Control, ownership, this is the making of intimate partner violence. I unfriended him on Facebook and never talked to him again.

I am grateful to know the flags. I was very close to investing in this relationship. I do not want to be his sponsor, counselor, life saver, or victim. I only want to love and be loved. I want a companion, a best friend, who is not on the verge of suicide, who does not manipulate using suicide as a weapon of control, and who has their own income. Is that too much to desire?

14 ONLINE DATING RESUMES - 2010

The loneliness sets in every year or so and I go back to online dating and looking up. If it's a numbers game, then the odds increase every time I take the risk of responding to a flirt or to meet someone for coffee or a meal. "I will find my Prince" became my mantra. I refuse to sit back waiting for Mr. Right to plop in front of me, I will put myself out there. I will risk my turn at rejection, take a chance and date again. I can love, I want to love, I will find another who offers a spark and potential for a future together, forever, on a white horse riding off into the sunset.

Yet, the adult part of me knows it's the Cinderella illusion. The fairy tale every girl is taught to dream. I observe friends and family and know that eventually the Velcro stage in the beginning doesn't last. Not only do couples become annoyed with one another, sometimes they despise each other, and most of the people I know end up divorced and bitter. Even knowing that, I long for the commitment with the fairy tale ending. I want to have a one-in-a-million story where love grows for the next fifty years, and adoration never wanes. Only at this point in my life forever is likely to be twenty years and my best years are fading fast!

I do notice this about myself. I spend a few days or a week with others and they get on my nerves. It doesn't mean I break up with them, I just pay attention and resist the urge to act on my first thoughts of annoyance. The irritability comes and goes, and it does pass. I'm not saying I don't speak up when I need to about other people's behaviors that cross my boundaries. I am talking about my annoyances about things that don't matter; teeth grinding, someone blowing their nose, incessant humming or leaving the toilet seat up. When I'm irritated at little things, it's about me. I need to refocus and find some roses to smell. I also need to acknowledge that I can be annoying to others even when I'm totally okay with my sniffling and snorting, farting, and driving like a granny.

Then those same people with little annoyances show up in such big ways. They help when my car breaks down or my house needs repair. They call or take me to dinner or celebrate my existence on my birthday. They tell me they love me from a heartfelt place that I know is beyond words. They take me to or from the hospital or clinic when I'm vulnerable and need their help. I am reminded it's all worth it. That's when I know I want a partner beyond a doubt. I am capable of letting go of annoyances and talking about difficult topics. I can ask for help and be open to loving another. Most of the time, I'm even willing to speak up when things need to be articulated.

It doesn't appear that I'll be meeting my prince charming anytime soon. I need to accept things as they are.

I live in Seattle where the reputation is that of the "Seattle Freeze". The people here are nice, but the boundaries are so thick. Dating in Washington is different from the Midwest.

When I travel to Michigan, Wisconsin, or Iowa, cab drivers ask me out. I've been living here in the PNW for decades and don't recall ever being asked out unless I've been visiting the dating sites.

Except once when I was asked out by a guy walking down the street in Capitol Hill. He sent me a picture of his penis. I deleted his number.

I notice the culture difference when I'm on an elevator. It is so inappropriate to look at or talk to others in this space. My hunches become magnified when confined with Seattleites in a small, cold, metal box. Unwritten rules exist in the PNW to not look around and certainly not talk to a stranger in an elevator or even on the street for that matter. Social norms make meeting guys naturally hard in Seattle and Portland.

I want to be at peace with me and all the loving people and pets I have in my life. I lost my chocolate lab, Lucky, and now I am grateful for the two dogs I tried to replace her with. This includes my very cute, ungodly yappy Papillon puppy, Bear. Then there's my fear aggressive nipper, a terrier-mix and my protector, Buddy. I truly love them even when Bear does his high pitch wine and Buddy bites my friends. However, it is difficult to be grateful for what I don't have.

For instance, having a partner who is too annoying to love and too loving not to adore. Hum. Is that what I think? Do I believe it is not possible to have a mate who doesn't annoy me? Maybe that's why I'm alone. I don't want to spend my life being irritated. What a stupid thought, like that is my only choice. Are all partners like my annoying but loveable Papillion? Cute as they get and sassy as can be? He's growing on me. I suppose if I had a mate I'd get used to their imperfections and love them anyway, too. They'd have to be pretty darn cute though.

Seriously, though, I really can change my mind and not react negatively to annoyances that I could blow off as insignificant. I can work on that with my dogs that yap and bite. I'll focus on peace and love and redirect. I will love myself and be okay, even thrive, without a partner. I'll accept things as they are, acceptance is key. I need to be okay with myself before I can be okay with anyone else, including my sweet and sometimes annoying doggies.

Another year goes by, maybe two, lost count. I got back on OurTime.com, the over 50's site. At least the men on OurTime aren't players like those who frequent those other sites. The wham-bam-thank-you-ma'am types that take advantage of the young, naive girls who shave their pubic hairs to resemble a child, and don't have an opinion except their partners.

I spent my entire life until I was thirty being one of those girls, in some ways. I didn't realize I had a voice or that I could use it, I just stayed stoned and smiled a lot. I smoked what you smoked, voted for your candidate (I would have if I'd ever got to the ballot box), believed as you did, and considered you my soulmate. No, I like OurTime.com because I perceive it to mean the men found there are interested in dating women over fifty, not young girls they think they can manipulate and show off like a trophy.

Sharing life's final chapter with someone to love,

who might even be in my age range is more my style. I have hope that I will find someone looking for what I seek, a partner to live out my golden years that admires me and whom I adore. The gratitude will be mutual and the respect never ending, I just know it. It's so close, at my fingertips, and I've been waiting all my life for this. Icing on the cake is the romantic proposal, preferably on a Black Stallion, or white, I don't believe I'm that picky.

I hate to admit that as I get older, hopefully wiser, and certainly not quite as naïve, I wonder if OurTime is where those shady men go to find a successful woman. One who is ready to retire and whom they can manipulate out of her retirement. Perhaps I've watched too much crime TV or Dr. Phil. Am I an older wise woman or a Debbie Downer, the eternal skeptic? I only know I'm changing. I am desperately trying to hang on to hope. I could meet a good guy, one who has his own retirement, and we could ride off into the sunset of my imagination forever after never having to be worried about money or being scammed again. We would ride off on his stallion. This forever after is getting shorter.

Could I learn to ride a horse I could ride off into the sunset on? Ugg. I haven't been too successful with horseback riding, but it's so beautiful. It just seems a bit late in life. I'd probably break a few bones if I fell off like I did in my younger years. Each and every attempt I made to command the giant majestic creature to carry me through the valley I came to regret. It's not that I wasn't graceful. I wasn't aggressive enough to kick their sides and tell them whose boss. They knew it and threw me off every time. My bones take longer to heal now. I might have to start imagining riding off in a Lyft instead of a stallion. Or we could stroll off into the sunset with our walkers.

15 ROBERT – OCTOBER 2013

My mother died the week I got sober in 1992. My niece died at 29 years old suddenly in 2008. I lost my dad in 2009, my oldest sister in 2011, and my older brother in 2012. Throw in a favorite dog who died after thirteen years, a couple of sponsees who died from illness and relapses, and three sponsees who relapsed after twenty years who gave up their magnificent clean and sober lives. I will attest to the fact that it is possible to grieve and not relapse.

I took a couple years off from online dating to work on feeling the feelings and letting them pass. Eventually, I got tired of feeling the feelings and got back online.

I met a man named Robert, from OurTime.com, one night after work at Starbucks. He was already seated with a coffee, so it was clear I was on my own paying for my beverage. I have no problem with that, though I have begun noticing. On one hand, I'm sure if I was the man and expected to pay for every coffee date I went on, I'd be broke at this rate and stop doing it. On the other hand, I tend to notice if someone asks you out and can't afford coffee, well, it screams of cheapskate. Or poverty. I've been both and don't admire these qualities in myself nor seek them from my future partner.

I realized during the date that Robert is also a medical social worker. We have this in common. I start to perk up from an otherwise kind of boring beginning.

It's nice to have a connection right away and a focus for conversation. We have so many stories we could share. Since my job is managing the crisis line, and he used to work in the ER, there are some themes that can serve as stress relief when talking with another social worker. Perhaps even laughing about how crazy those full moon shifts can be. I need this in my life.

I need to laugh at the insanity of situations that show up when people are in crisis so I can de-stress, debrief, and laugh. Naturally, I would not give identifying details to a partner or anyone else, mind you. Without this ability to let go and laugh after the workday is done, the intensity of being a first responder, even over the phone, can have the impact of secondary, vicarious trauma.

Robert's first story about working in the ER and how he'd made a list that he handed out to people in crisis…left me stunned. He was proudly telling me that he gave the list to people having suicidal thoughts or having just tried to take their own life, of actual lethal ways someone could really kill themselves.

Yes, the list had mostly easy to access means and directions on how to make it work. He did not like people who were desperately seeking attention and/or practicing the real thing. It was no surprise that he was fired from his ER position.

This left me dumbfounded. I'm unsure if he was

paying attention, but my face said it all. Are you serious? Oh, he was, and so joyful about his clever solution for his suicidal patients. No, I'm not looking for the murderer type disguised as a social worker named Robert. I didn't pretend to have finished my tea. I just got up and left. Hopefully, he was asking himself, "Was it something I said"?

16 ETHAN - DECEMBER 2013

Ethan contacted me on OurTime. "Mr. Hopeful". I loved that. I can assume he is not a player; this is the place to find partners over fifty. It puts me at ease that unlike PlentyOfFish.com, people are not just looking for a brief sexual encounter. His profile says he is looking for a serious relationship. He's very good looking for a fifty-one-year-old, he is 6'4", he earns great money, and he doesn't drink. Now I'm feeling hopeful. The best part is that we live in the same town, so it's convenient and exciting.

After texting for a couple of days Ethan and I exchange numbers and plan to chat. While he's got a bit of a sexy edge to his correspondence, he's playful and I like that. We text and text and text. I want him to ask me to coffee, the typical next move, which is not happening after several days. He's texting me morning noon and night and yet, no action toward moving on toward the next step. Strange. I am having a blast playing with him, but I'd rather know who I am playing with. Still, I am going to see how long it takes him to ask me out. We certainly have established a connection.

After ten days of ongoing texting, I am beginning to think that is all he wants. Texting and the illusion of a relationship. A fantasy relationship. This is so strange, and I can't stand going on this way. He's texting me one night about how lonely he is without a woman by his side and I finally text back, "then why don't you ask the kind and patient woman on the other end of this phone out for coffee?" The two-by-four tactic tends to work. Naturally, he asked me out to dinner.

I was excited, but a little skeptical. I don't know if he's married or what his deal is. Why is someone who's online dating not actually interested in dating?

We went to a nice Mexican restaurant, La Hacienda in Marysville. I dress up and wear my boots with heels knowing how tall he is, which is smart. He is really tall. Oh, and even better looking than his photos. While we are staring into one another's eyes over dinner, with exceptionally wide grins, he says he doesn't drink and he's in a recovery program. This is so awesome. He does a little role play of his drunken days and talks about being kicked out of the Alano hall showing up drunk and acting the fool. I can just see it. We absolutely connect and laugh together about the absurdity of acting like jerks in the past.

I'm not seeing a fool at this moment. I am sitting across from a man who is proud of his sobriety, states he has a sponsor, reports loving his management job at Boeing, and who just bought a house in Marysville. The new puppy he just bought is his focus since his kids are grown and he's been divorced for years. I take note of the pain he has concerning his children that he doesn't want to talk about. I assume it has something to do with neglect from his drinking days. He had twenty years, relapsed, and has more than a year again. I can compare my twenty-three years of sobriety and see a similarity with where we are in our programs. I wish he had more sobriety, but I am excited we share this lifestyle of recovery because it is so much a part of my life.

Dinner went smoothly. He walks me to my car, hugs me, there is electricity, and he walks away. I am on fire. We get home and text one another how fun it was to meet. He tells me how much he wanted to kiss me. Really? Me too! He lets me know next time he won't just walk away. I told him I'm going to hold him to his promise.

The next night he wanted to meet for dinner again. Well, okay, that would be great. He takes me to Christiano's, the fabulous Italian restaurant in town that is one of my favorites. He said to order anything that I want on the menu. This is a relief; I like to order what I want but don't always want to get something too expensive when someone else is buying. I don't remember my meal, but I remember how great the conversation was. I remember the anticipation of the upcoming kiss. I was feeling tingly all over and felt like a schoolgirl.

After dinner, he walked me outside, stood in front of Christiano's near my car and gave me the kiss of a lifetime. It was sexy and heartfelt, it left me wanting more. Wow. I didn't want to leave. I can count the decades since I felt hope and passion, and I didn't want it to end. I'm instantly wet with desire and all I can think of is, 'don't go'. But the good girl in me is going to do the right thing and try to build a relationship with this very hot guy, my neighbor, Ethan. Sexy, edgy, Ethan. "Mr. Hopeful" as his profile describes.

I got in my car and went home. Again, we text and

text and desire more, but we are adults and continue to build a bond. It's Christmas week and we didn't make future plans, but I was so ready to see him again I could hardly stand it. The next day he invites me to his house to watch the Seattle Seahawks playoffs as they head toward the Super Bowl. I'm not into the game, but the entire state is lit up on Seahawk fever and I understand it.

I decided to bring him a party in a bag since he'd bought me dinner twice. On break at work, I ran to the grocery store and bought shrimp, cocktail sauce, cream cheese, crackers, salami and Havarti, grapes, veggies, dips, Chex mix, chips, etc., etc., etc. I went way overboard but thought he could think of me as he ate leftovers. I was so glad to see his cute little house, see that he isn't married, meet his adorable puppy, and watch the game with him. It was so fun. He was noticeably clean and well dressed, and his house was immaculate. He lit a candle, curled up with me on the couch. He began kissing and fondling me.

I do not know how we lasted until halftime before hitting his bedroom, but he was irresistible, and I was a freaking gummy bear. I have not had sex since I can remember, let alone sex like that. He missed the Seahawks playoffs.

I didn't fully understand the significance of that gesture until I became a Seahawks fan many years later.

I did not feel fifty-five and he did not appear to be fifty-one. We were like school kids on fire with hormones raging. Only we'd had some experience to draw from and it made the whole thing so much better. It was ravaging lust. Two people totally in the right place at the right time doing the right thing. It was fun, honest, beautiful, and memorable. I really, really, really, really like Ethan.

Single and Sober: Who Found My Slipper?

He invited me to stay overnight but I must work the next morning, so I said no. I need to put our food away, go home and feed my dog. I will text or call him tomorrow, Christmas Eve. Ethan has plans with his family, so we'll talk as we're able.

He was gentle as he slowly backed away. I never saw him again. He stopped returning texts or calls. I wanted to run to his house and scream at him, but I let it go. I mean where were we supposed to go from there? I was envisioning a life together, where we went to meetings and hung out with people in the program. A life where we talked about being all that we could be and sought through prayer and meditation a higher power that ran our lives. A life that was rooted in spiritual principles and giving to others.

In retrospect, I did get caught up in lust and I was in a fantasy land. I don't think Ethan had a program at all, despite what he told me. He never went to meetings and after relapsing less than a year ago, he really wasn't connected in the fellowship. This should have been a huge red flag for me. I wanted him to be someone he was not. Still, I don't understand how or why someone looking for a partner would play these kinds of games on OurTime.com, the site for over fifty-year-olds. It really sucks. My sponsor and others say, hey, enjoy it for what it was. You needed that.

No. No one needed that. I cannot stand the pretentiousness. If I had thought I'd never see him again, I would not have gone there with him. Sure, I knew sex was premature, but I was deceived. That is not the only thing I wanted, and it wasn't okay to leave me feeling used. But it was fun for an evening, despite all that. It was the following year that sucked when I couldn't trust men, again. I don't want to wear scars or be bitter, but men like this take a knife into my side a little deeper each time I have experiences like this. I lose faith in humanity, that people, men in particular, can be honorable. It would be different if I was in it for a one-night stand, like in the old days when I was drinking or using drugs. This was not a set up for a meaningless evening together. There were some clues, but there was also deception.

UPDATE - NOVEMBER 2015

Tonight, I was driving home late after a windstorm hit the suburbs with significant force. After dodging tree limbs and darting through intersections without traffic lights, I made it close to home before deciding to stop at the one restaurant in town that looked open. Ordering food to go, along with half of Marysville, it took over an hour to order and get what food they had left. Wasn't I surprised when two years after that wild fling with my neighbor I turned around and spotted Ethan in line behind me. I tried to hide in a corner of this overly lit teriyaki joint, with simply nowhere but the bathroom to run.

I reminded myself I did nothing wrong; I felt sorry for him, and I never hated him. I can wear my head high. I began talking to a stranger, laughing, making chit chat about the weather. The Korean man at the counter yelled to the line of people still coming through the front door that they were now out of chicken. Ethan made a beeline for the door. I'm not positive he saw me, but my inclination is that he did. He left with his head low and tail between his legs. He can't feel good about himself, and by the way, he wasn't nearly as attractive or sexy as I remember. So long Ethan. I'm not feeling bitter, just awkward. Could be because I had sex with you before getting to know you, and that is not how I act to feel the best about myself.

UPDATE - SPRING 2017

Sitting at the six am meeting with a member of the fellowship, Jolene, chit chatting after the meeting when she starts to inquire about how I know Ethan. She noticed we were Facebook friends and said she was his friend, too. Casually, she mentioned she'd been with him, too. She slept with him and assumed I had sex with him. Really? What? Whoa. That was a first. Yeah, he's a player, alright. She smiled and added, "heck of a good lover, though, huh?"

UPDATE - SEPTEMBER 2022

Insight comes slow but steady. Many years after that night I began to see where I used Ethan, too. Now, I'm not trying to take on his behavior as my fault by any means. If I want health in my life, I must become healthy. This 12-Step work is not for sissies. Here's the part I played in that whirlwind romance with Ethan.

First, I urged him to take me out when he wasn't asking me out. Next, I encouraged him to take me out a second time and to kiss me when he was resisting. Finally, I was prime material for going all the way when we went to his house for the football game. He did say later that he only intended on making out.

True or not, I was a bit eager. I was not okay getting hot and heavy and stopping there. I encouraged him to use me, in fact, I used him. I hate admitting this but it's true. I ignored all the signs out of lust. He gave an inch; I took a mile. We were both left feeling icky and used.

He kept saying afterward, "oops, I didn't mean to go that far, I just meant to make out". I was too eager, call it ripe, lonely, horny, call it what you will, but I had no desire to pull back. I was an equal opportunity user, too. Oops. I should be more kind to myself and to Ethan's in the future.

I learned that I need to pay more attention to the message being sent, not just how I feel and act. I was so excited, but I'm not sure that he felt that way too. He was excited, mind you, but I'm referring to his emotional state. In retrospect, he tried to control his own urges and I pushed him to go for it when it's possible he wasn't ready. Who knows why he was refraining, but I totally missed that.

I do wonder if he is a sex addict in recovery, without following a program. I'm sometimes blind to the obvious when my emotions are running high. I now know that there are two people at play here and my feelings do prevent me from looking at the bigger picture clearly. I will pay more attention to the other part of the equation should this type of situation arise again in my life, pun intended.

Perhaps my intentions of having a long-term relationship were more honorable. In the end, I was not the upstanding character I thought myself to be until this period of reflection. It didn't feel right in my gut, though, and I needed to work my Steps on this experience. Insight was slow to come to me, difficult to accept, but very important to learn. I keep working the Steps, cleaning house, and getting restored to sanity. One date at a time.

Single and Sober: Who Found My Slipper?

17 PAUL – FEBRUARY 2014

Paul walked into Starbucks with his eyes sparkling and his cowboy boots shining. I'm not typically attracted to the cowboy, but there was something classy about this man, simple, and admirable. Paul presents himself with honor and dignity, a hard worker who loves rock music. He is a fly fisherman from Montana. He has an instant crush on me. Paul's very pleased with what he's seeing and isn't afraid to show it. He's amazed at my accomplishments and the feeling is mutual. We went next door to a diner for dinner after talking for an hour effortlessly. He offers to buy dinner, opens the restaurant door for me, and acts like a gentleman throughout the evening.

The next day is Valentine's Day, and he invites me out to a nice restaurant on the water. I decided to check if the place is only seating with reservations. As it turns out it was too late to reserve a table, which he had not done. I called around, contacted him, and let him know we couldn't get in at the first place. However, we now have reservations on the Puget Sound waterfront at another nice place. He didn't seem too offended that I'd called in advance, and he said he thought I was smart for checking.

I brought Paul a packet of sweetheart candies and made him a card asking if he would be my Valentine. He was impressed and once again, we had the greatest evening talking and starting to get to know one another. I'm beginning to like his shiny boots and belt buckle. I could see the serenity behind his passion for fly fishing and could see myself relaxing on the river with him in Montana. He's getting close to retiring.

Paul had a bit of energy around his divorce some years back. Turns out he owned a business that his wife worked at, too. The way he tells it, she operated the books. Paul says his wife neglected to pay the IRS for a long time. When he found out he was so far behind he had to close the shop and go to work for another company so he could pay back his debt. It's been over a decade and now he hopes to retire in the not-too-distant future.

When he realized how far in debt with the IRS he was, Paul relapsed after twenty years of sobriety. He went on a three-year bender and moved to Eastern Washington. It was there he met his last girlfriend, who was from Western Washington. They lived together until a year ago when she couldn't stop drinking and he asked her to move out. He was in love with her and admitted this was hard. He joined Alanon to heal from his role in the insanity after fruitless attempts to make her stop drinking.

Paul has some baggage, but he seems stable all in all. He appears to be working on his issues. I love that he's in recovery and I can see us going to meetings and events together in the future. He invited me over for pizza one night and to play guitar. He played bass. We have a similar taste in music, and we really hit it off. It was so fun! He explained he likes sex, but he does not want to have sex until he's ready (hey, wait, that's my line!). I let him know I feel the same, no hurry, I'd like to just get to know him better. Yeeha, on the same page. Relax. Let's have fun.

We started playing. I take him to the Mountain Loop Hwy and introduce him to my chocolate lab, Lucky. He shows me how to read the river, ooh that was sexy. Love a guy in nature who can read the river. That was a first. I like his calm energy and the way he lights up speaking about his cabin in Montana. His home is simply beautiful, I can only imagine the cabin is quaint, too.

He continues to invite me over to his house. We ate pizza on many occasions and visited. We talked about music. One night, I'm so freaking nervous backing out of his driveway when I was leaving (backing up is a phobia I have). I go slow, waiting to feel where the gravel drive stops, and the paved road starts, so I can turn out of the driveway and leave.

However, the smooth blacktop never comes. I back up and back up and back up until I feel my back wheels go over an incline and I'm at a 90-degree angle staring up at the stars. Oh, I just hate it when things like this happen! I back up some more to straighten out the front wheels knowing I'm screwed. I back up a little more to get momentum, try gunning the engine, and my car gets halfway up the three-foot incline before falling back down again. I gun it again and only fall deeper into the grass, wheels tearing up the neighbor's lawn, car wiggling around like a dancer on meth. I cannot fathom just how I'm going to get out of this mess.

I tuck my tail between my legs and go back up to

Paul's door. I am appearing as a damsel in distress. Dang, I hate this. I knock lightly. I can see his TV is off now and I wonder if he's in the shower or bed. I just can't do it; I can't swallow my pride and keep knocking. I'm too embarrassed. I leave and go back to my car. I will tell him I did this, tomorrow, but I will rescue my car from his neighbor's lawn tonight and I will pay for sodding, dirt, or for some John Deere tractor to come level out his lawn. I will right the wrong.

Only right now I need to figure out how to get up over that embankment to the road and go home. It's late, I'm tired, Paul's in bed and the neighbors' lights are all off. I stare at the property and try to figure it out. If I drive parallel to the road to the end of the neighbor's property I could probably excel and angle my car to get up onto the road. The only negative thing I would do is leave tire tracks alongside a quarter acre of grass and that's not as bad as digging holes in his yard like I've already done. I tried it, it works, yay. I went home and slept.

The next day I called Paul and told him what happened. I let him know he can tell his neighbor I am the culprit, but I am good for making it right. Paul laughs, says "it's no biggie", and that he'll talk to his neighbor. He was disappointed that I didn't keep knocking and let him help me. I took note of this for future reference.

I felt better about the incident until he said his neighbor was a judge. There was something about that that did not feel right. Judges are not neutral, they judge. I didn't want to be judged. Later, Paul assessed the damage and said there wasn't any. I do not believe that. Still, I never went to talk to the neighbor and make it right, that was wrong of me. I do need to address that or right the wrong of something equivalent in the future.

Back to Paul. Things are going along so sweetly. He's texting me, taking me to nice places, relaxing on the weekend, it's super fun. We talk about recovery, but he only goes to Alanon when he's hurting, not routinely. Then he starts acting hot and cold. It's so weird.

On the weekends he wants to get together, but when I try to pinpoint which day or night, he is vague and non-committal. One weekend he wanted to spend Friday, Saturday, and Sunday together and the next weekend he put me off Friday to Saturday. Saturday to Sunday.

I was being strung along. He is not getting together with me and is full of lame excuses. The next weekend he's all crazy about me again, fun on Friday, music on Saturday, mountains on Sunday. The following weekend he's absent again. It's all so strange. I finally asked him to decide if he wants this or he doesn't. The indecision is wearing me down. He said he wanted it, he begged me to give him another chance, and pleaded how much he really wanted this. Then he proceeded to ignore me and my texts for a week.

On that Saturday when I would normally be at his house, I decided to drive by his property. I've prepared a whole song list we could practice from. I'm excited to play music with him and feeling rejected because he is not responding, again. I act like a stalker as I head to his house, but I have no intention of ringing his doorbell. I only want to see what he's doing when he's not with me. Is he depressed and at home alone on a Saturday night or is he not home and out playing with someone other than me? I'm curious to find out more as things were not adding up for me. Hot, cold, crazy, insane.

Single and Sober: Who Found My Slipper?

I was extremely surprised to find he was home and that he was not alone. Her car was all tucked into his driveway up toward the boat, probably just like she used to park. The lights are dim but just enough to see the shadow of two bodies in his bedroom walking around. Seriously? The ex is not an ex. He did tell me he still loved her. He was going to Alanon to deal with her, the alcoholic. Dang, I can be so blind. I want to believe that I was the catalyst for his realizing that he still loved her. I also want to believe this was their first time together since last year, so the story he told me, and the real one were the same. I am naive, but a diehard optimist, too.

Paul did let me know two days later that he wasn't ready to get into a relationship with me at this time. I was glad I learned the truth, especially the part he left off. It helped to know it was his love for her and not his distaste for me, which I would have questioned otherwise. Perhaps I was lying to myself, and he was playing us both the whole time. That's my naive side. If that's the case he's going to die of a heart attack soon from all the anxiety. Still, I think if he was a sleaze bag he would have been trying to get in my pants. Instead, when I did see him, he treated me like a queen and spent time getting to know me. I respect Paul and chose to believe he just couldn't get rid of his bad habit: the still very sick alcoholic.

UPDATE - WINTER 2018

I ran into Paul at a monthly family recovery event out on the Swinomish Indian Reservation. My heart pounded fast, and I wanted to hide. I think I remember being cool with him, but I'm confused at that moment if I should be pissed off or not. I'm embarrassed because he's with the cute blonde, the alcoholic, the not so ex-ex. Oh, it makes sense they would attend this meeting together because it's family oriented with both AA and Alanon speakers. Hey, at least they could be working a program.

I passed him by when he was alone, but he didn't recognize me. I'm so relieved. Just a little bummed, too. I feel invisible at times and think I need to be more boisterous. I saw him a few more times the following year. Still, no recognition. Not even a glimpse. It's too weird.

UPDATE - NOVEMBER 2022

I had the urge to attend a meeting one Saturday morning that I don't usually attend. It's very early in the morning and cold out, so I argue with myself about leaving the house or going back to bed. For some strange reason I'm drawn to go, so I drag myself up and get dressed. I chose the cuter of my two sweaters I contemplate wearing. I picked my brown suede knee high boots rather than my new, but ugly, white sneakers. I don't know why. It's so early many people show up in PJs, it's no fashion statement crowd like the Friday and Saturday night 12-Step meetings can appear to be.

I'm off to the early morning breakfast meeting, on time, a rarity for me this early. Immediately, I spotted a few of my home group members from the Sunday meeting and I feel at ease. The sign-in sheet is moving past me and needs someone to give it to the Chairperson, so I stand up and at the same time a guy near me stands up to do the same.

There we are. Nose to nose. It's Paul. I don't give

him a chance not to know me. I nod, "Paul", I say, in recognition. He grins and nods back. I'm so glad I wore my cute boots and sharp sweater is my first thought. Is she here is my next thought. I look around. Nope, but he's a regular here, all the home group members seem to know him.

I act all sly and friendly like I am holding no resentments, which I'm not so I'm not acting, just nervous. He is called on and shares about the weather, literally, talking about the room we are in that has no heat. I get the impression the meeting room has been cold all week. I'm not bothered by it, but it helped to have worn a sweater and a heavy coat. I get called on to share my experience, strength, and hope. Luckily, I'm able to think straight. Glad I was able to practice seeing him a few times a few years back, it helped me to prepare for this moment. I shared about the topic and made a few jokes. I left them laughing and spoke from the heart. Not bad for the first thing in the morning with a sort of ex in the room.

After the meeting Paul came right up to me and asked if he could speak to me for a minute. I said "yes, sure" and led him to a corner in the room. He got close to my ear and said, "I owe you an apology and an amends". I listened. He went on, "I was not at a good point in my life…I was afraid…it was fear". I told him I really appreciated his acknowledging that and I knew he wasn't in the right headspace. He cut me off, "I was at a very low point, I was in fear, I was afraid…". I let him know I held no resentments, and I accepted his apology.

He went on to talk about those few times we got together and the fear he had starting a relationship with me. He never mentioned the woman, his addiction. He talked about having been buying guitars ever since and kept saying "I don't know who I want to be". I'm unsure if he meant a guitar player or bass player, a musician, or who he wanted to be in life. It doesn't matter. I talked about writing songs, and he acted surprised. I bragged, yes, I did, about having released a CD of all original songs, which impressed him. I guess I wanted him to swallow what he missed out on. I made that CD long before I met him, but it's not my style to brag about it in the first few dates.

I was disappointed that we didn't get to see where things led, and I let him know that. I had been so inspired by him that I wrote out a song list of twenty songs we could work out as a Duo, but he canceled that date, and I never got a chance to play with him again. I notice that he still didn't mention the woman that was a significant part of the story. Regardless of where his life is now, it will never be anything other than being comfortable sitting across the table from him, in a meeting. Omission is a lie. I know the story has more depth and I feel like he is lying. A cute, incapable of telling the whole truth, storyteller. Best of luck to you, Paul. See ya around.

UPDATE – JANUARY 2023 BOBBY AND PAUL

Another friend, Bobby, sobered up fourteen months ago after I took him to a lot of meetings. He became clear-headed enough to notice the improvements in his life. He started drinking at the age of nine and stayed drunk or high until last year and he was then in his 50s. His birth mother was a Native American woman who was alcoholic and abused him severely.

Single and Sober: Who Found My Slipper?

Ellen is my best friend. Her family adopted Bobby as a baby. Ellen moved out of state recently and hated leaving her brother alone in WA. She considered it her job to help raise Bobby who has fetal alcohol syndrome. She'd always looked after him but had reached out to me to help keep an eye on him since she couldn't when she moved away.

Bobby and I had a special relationship since I picked up the slack when Ellen left. He considers me his aunt. He filled my void of not having my BFF Ellen around and I was amazed to watch him get sober, despite all odds. He stayed in my guest room on and off, but often preferred being homeless like he was used to doing for a lot of his adult life.

I was disappointed in the men in the fellowship because none of the guys he asked would sponsor him. Granted, he was living in a cardboard box, a refrigerator box. Those were only the nights when he would get caught and kicked out of his storage unit. He has a heart of gold but comes across like he's still using drugs. He drags his words and has overgrown and unwashed hair most of the time. His mind wanders a lot, and he tends to go on and on when he is called on to share in meetings. He talks about many things, often forgetting to acknowledge his experience with recovery.

People running the groups must rein him in and interrupt him to keep order in the meeting. Everyone seems to think he's using drugs or drinking when his mental illness goes untreated, or his cognitive deficits become noticeable. Lord knows I tried to help him get the right medication and counseling going, but he could never quite show up for his appointments, even sober.

Bobby is renting a home about six hours away but came back to the Everett area for a visit. He stayed at my house last night. We were both up for the day and ready to hit a meeting at the break of dawn. I decided to take him to a meeting where he may run into some of the men he met last year going to meetings in this area. Unfortunately, those familiar faces were not there this week. Instead, we ran into Paul who is all nicely tucked in next to Barb, possibly his newest girlfriend.

As we sit across from them it is occurring to me how this looks. I'm walking in at sunrise with a guy whose hair is all ruffled up, grinning from ear to ear, missing all his front teeth. I am guessing it looks like I picked up this newcomer from some ally and I'm rubbing some kind of vengeance in Paul's face. I don't care how things look anymore. This is one of my gifts of getting older and of recovering. What other people think about me is none of my business. I don't have to worry about what others think of me, what a freedom that is! I let go of needless anxiety.

Naturally, like most meetings, everybody gets called on except Bobby, whose turn came up just prior to ending the meeting. He shares nothing about his sobriety, his experience getting sober, or the benefits of now having a home. Instead, he's talking about something or other when he blurts out, "but you know who thinks I'm cool? She does," pointing at me. "She really likes me; she thinks I'm great!"

I do, seriously. But not in the way everyone was probably thinking. He's doing great not drinking. He's changing his life, I am in awe. We respect one another and we are both clear that I'm like his aunt and he needs a haircut. Finally, the chairperson cuts him off so we can close the meeting on time. Life in recovery is amusing to say the least.

I've heard it said if you can't break up with someone you've dated from the fellowship and be able to sit across from them in a meeting you are setting yourself up for a relapse. I feel confident I can sit across from Paul and it will put neither of us ill at ease.

Bobby ended up relapsing and keeps telling me he's heading for treatment. I hope one day he makes it, I'd hate for his ending to resemble my friend Teddy's. Bobby has potential he has never even explored. Prayer helps me "do something". Good wishes, good vibes, God does for us that which we cannot do for ourselves. If only we get out of the way and let the miracle happen.

18 DON – JULY 2015

In 2014 when I was sent to MI to do some work, my middle sister threw a party for her kids' birthdays. I was immediately attracted to a single man who came to her party. Turns out this is the Don that my sister talked about so often, a friend of hers and her fiancé's. Don handed me a birthday card when he arrived, which was sweet, especially since it wasn't my birthday, it was my niece and nephew's celebration.

He may have heard it was my 21st recovery birthday, also, but we weren't celebrating that at this party. He was flirting at the food table, and it made me confused because the card he gave me was signed by himself and a woman, perhaps his wife or child? I flirted back but made it a point to ask my sister about him later.

During the evening of laughter, games, and stories, I found Don checking me out a few times. It felt flattering since simple acts of flirting have lessened as I've grown older. Funny how flirting gradually disappears after a woman becomes a mother and is extinct by the time she is a grandmother. Guys of all ages flirt. Makes me think guys only want little girls. We live in a sick society.

Never-the-less I began to think maybe Don was single, but I wondered why he signed a card from himself and a female. I pulled my sister aside and asked about him. She told me he had been separated for a few years now, but it was complicated. He still lived in the basement of their house. Hum. That's odd, I thought, but he is kind of cute.

Late in the evening we somehow got started talking about what I did for a living. I made the mistake of talking about my part time job as a crisis triage clinician doing suicide prevention work. Several of the tail end party guests started to open up about their depression. Don told me about his father and brothers' suicides.

Oh my gosh, this is a guy who has been through so much loss, I can't imagine. No wonder he is part of my sisters' 12-Step fellowship and he's committed to healing. That would be something I would never "get over". I liked the way Don talked about his mother and her new husband that he said was not an abuser like Don's father had been.

Knowing what I know I cannot help but think that Don could be an abuser. He's certainly learned about abusive behavior from his father. But what I'm seeing is a sensitive, caring man, who could also be the victim of his dad. Victims of violent abuse can grow up knowing it's not okay and fight against domestic violence throughout their lives. Some will cope with the memories and lasting effects by using alcohol or other drugs. However, there are some children exposed to violence who learn to control their partners and will go to any length to do this, including being violent.

My heart goes out to Don & his mom. I don't know

him or the pain he's experienced, but I know he's doing the right thing by going to meetings with my sister and talking about his loss tonight. I can't imagine ever talking that "out", but life would be a series of talking it "through" if that's even possible. It's got to be so sad to lose your father and brother and both by suicide.

I clicked with Don. I can't remember how we decided to become Facebook friends, but we did. In fact, Don joined Facebook to communicate with me, and I walked him through it. We talked on the phone and texted for months after we met at my niece and nephews' birthday party. It was fun, until it started to get serious. Don was playful, always texting me lyrics of songs and I would finish the song or come up with a new one. I had such a blast giggling at what we came up with and the audacity of some lyrics to strike chords and express feelings. I loved this. It was a music era I was familiar with, fun, and sexy at times. Ooh la la.

After a while I started to have growing feelings and Don's moving out of the basement of his wife's house just wasn't in his radar. I asked what he wanted, "to explore the gardens?", "to plant himself with or near someone?" or to "get married again?". He said he wanted to explore. I thought if I'd been married for thirty years I would too, and that's honest & right where he needs to be, so I let him.

I told him I didn't think he was available and that I should quit texting because my heart was getting involved. He understood and left me alone. Sure, he continued to *like* all my postings on Facebook, but that was the extent of it. He was respectful and backed off when I asked him to, a very good sign. I know the people who won't let you break up, even if you aren't going together, can be the potentially dangerous ones.

A year went by before my sister and her fiance' became engaged and began to make wedding plans. My sister wanted me to sing at her wedding, both in the ceremony and at the reception. She was planning a coffee house type of reception with the twenty musicians she knew, each playing one song. She had a favorite song she requested I sing in the ceremony, but she left it up to me to pick the song I played at her reception. I dug through the songs I knew and thought Stevie Nicks and Don Henley, "Leather and Lace" would be great. Only I needed a male to sing the Henley part.

Meanwhile, Don is posting pictures on Facebook of his new apartment, the freedom he is feeling having moved out, and how it was harder thinking about than making the move. He was moving on from his marriage and I was surprised and delighted. I sent him a text and asked if he sang and/or would be interested in singing at my sister's wedding. Knowing this would be risky, I mentally prepared for him to say no, be terrible, get stage fright, or not be able to remember the words. I am willing to risk it because it was all in fun. I could sing along, have him simply say the words, or just let it suck. He'd have only a couple lines and at worst it would be the fact that he was brave enough to try that would be fun, regardless. The element of surprise for the newlyweds would be fabulous.

Don was willing to learn the song. He was not afraid of the stage as he'd been giving readings at his church in front of 400 people regularly. He made it a point to commit and to not be afraid. We spent a couple months flirting on the phone, practicing on speaker phone (not recommended) and laughing at the lack of progress since we were constantly unable to hear the other or get in sync. We both knew it would work out fine after we spent a time or two practicing live, but it was nerve racking and exciting getting to know him better without expectations. Simple fun.

He wanted to take me to his favorite restaurant when we got together. We planned to practice in person when I flew to MI. He was hoping we could find the time to also take a bicycle ride together, as he is a cyclist. I let him know I needed to spend time with my great nephew, my great niece, my son, my sister & her fiancé, my nieces and nephews, a dear friend, and some of my seventy first cousins. Since the rehearsal for the wedding and the wedding itself meant half my days of my vacation were already pre-planned, I told him it may not happen. I agreed to go to dinner the night we rehearsed, but I doubted I'd get away again with non-stop company arriving until after the wedding. He said he understood.

I must say I was thrilled when I got to go see Don's apartment down river in Detroit, practice with him, and then go out to dinner. He had a very modern, spotless condo type of atmosphere, smartly decorated. It could have been right out of a magazine. I was truly happy for him. Practice went well, we laughed and rehearsed our butts off, and it was coming together. We did need another practice, though, and I let him know I would make the time for that, somehow.

Dinner at his favorite Mediterranean Restaurant was great; healthy and delicious. He had preplanned with the owners who knew this was an important meal for a special woman in his life. They treated us like royalty. It was very sweet. I didn't feel he had any expectations; he was a total gentleman. While I was hoping for a sweet and sexy kiss at the end of the night, he was polite and gracious. I knew that was good since we would be seeing each other a few times before the wedding and that could be awkward. Kisses always leave me wanting more.

After Ethan, I had no intention of sleeping with Don. Period. I would be okay with kissing though.

We were still planning to get together a few more times. We would try to fit in another practice, we'd see each other at the rehearsal dinner, and practice again the day of the wedding. I was very excited to spend time with Don as he was so attentive and let his attraction to me be transparent. Ooh la la. Even though he lives in MI, and I am in WA, he's thirty-one years at the Michigan Truck Plant, a Ford factory and he's beyond ready to retire. I'm from MI and my family and extended family live in the area. I could be happy in MI or in WA; my original home or my home by choice. Being with the right person I could make my home in either place.

I don't want to get ahead of myself. The chemistry is there, we are both attracted to one another like magnets, but I am wondering if he's truly separated from his wife, if they've divvied up their stuff, and if he's done playing the field. He's telling me he's ready, but I know actions speak louder than words. It is a very good sign that he moved out of his wife's house this year. My only expectation is that we will sing together at the wedding, and we will have fun doing it. We are well on our way. Oh, and a kiss would be nice. It's been a very long time.

As the week unfolded things got steamier between us. I threw an impromptu party at Teddy's one night so I could have an excuse to see him again without neglecting my family. It was a blast. He was wearing his emotions on his sleeve, crazy excited to see me, as I was him. We snuck in another practice after the bride and groom left Teddy's that night and wow, things were coming together nicely. Electric. It was very fun.

Teddy has been my friend for decades, he's gay and no threat to Don at all. Teddy and Don started to work together toward getting me to move to MI. Teddy is ready to put me up in his spare room at no cost, telling me I can take time to date Don and get to know him better. Don wants to finish up his job, take care of his aging mother and stepdad, and go through the final stages of his divorce. He wants to be ready to retire with me.

My friend Teddy and my possible boyfriend Don have it all worked out. Wow. I can't believe how good it feels to be wanted. It's weird to have the boys all figure out my life. It takes me back decades when my partner and father would pull that kind of behind-the-scenes decision making. How did the men in our society ever learn to think the women in their life's future is up to them? It's so wrong. Only this time it is what I want, too. When everything is in alignment it feels so right.

It's been twenty years of being alone, dating all the wrong guys, and it's like it has all been preparing me for this precious time in my life. A perfect moment in time for me to meet my soulmate. One who I'm crazy about and he is crazy about me. A guy who is conscientious about his faith, his health, his finances, his character, and someone in recovery for thirty some years who doesn't drink or do drugs. I could not have aligned this up any better. This is the perfect match for me. I can't stop smiling.

Single and Sober: Who Found My Slipper?

After the party, I walked Don to his car and the electricity between us was like fire. Still, he was a gentleman. We hugged, but he did not kiss me. He was so respectful, and I had a hard time not taking it further. I wanted to respect him and let him make the first move, I'm old school that way. I had a very difficult time holding back, though, with the wedding soon approaching I knew it'd be awkward if we went too far too soon. Dang, temptation is a powerful thing, especially since it's been twenty-four years since my last relationship to speak of. After Ethan, though, I am in no hurry to experience the wham bam thank-you ma'am again. Ever.

The wedding rehearsal and the lunch that followed were both delightful. Don and I sat by each other and supported one another through our times up on the altar, being each other's cheerleaders. It felt natural. I acted like I was singing to the bride and groom, but I was singing to Don. He seemed to enjoy my singing Kate Wolf song "Give Yourself to Love" and Don had raving reviews of my rendition. I rewrote the versus of the song to personalize it for the bride and groom.

Afterward, at lunch, we were not placed at the table of the happy couple, so we were able to spend the entire meal talking non-stop with each other. There was an occasional polite interaction with the other people at our table who all seemed to know one another, but we were engrossed with each other.

I can't remember what we talked about, but I do remember being buried in his deep, dark brown, glowing eyes. I wanted to pinch myself. Is this really happening? How did I go from thirty-two to fifty-six without a boyfriend to speak of? Was all that education, working, raising my son, and being alone just to prepare me for the beauty of waiting for true love like this? All those crazy speed dates, the coffee dates, the texting, the rejections, the rejecting…were they all part of the process in my quest for love? If so, this one moment in time was standing still and I was convinced in my soul that it was all worth it to feel the way I was feeling. I know this is it. We are meant to be together. Fin-na-ly. Thank-you, God.

The wedding day was awesome. We met at the church and hung out like we were an old married couple. He sat right up next to me, legs touching, staring into my eyes, his arm around my shoulder. My Aunt Pat and cousin Peggy were behind us and I'm certain they thought we were a couple. Don spoke like a true champion as he read what my sister asked him to read from the pulpit. He'd rehearsed it well and was able to keep eye contact with the audience and it was beautiful. His love for them shone through and contributed to their awesome ceremony.

When I sang, I was again singing to him and was giving it my all until I heard my sister say, "She sounds so great", which triggered me to forget the words and skip half of that verse. I somehow pulled it off, but the video will reveal the truth. It was wonderful to see my aunts and uncles, cousins, and especially to see the bride and groom share their vows and be like giggly school kids as they married for love and committed to their futures together.

I started to get nervous about doing the duet as we changed clothes and went to the park for the outdoor reception. Don offered to drive me, so we hung out the rest of the day together. I suddenly forgot my part of the song and panicked as we went through our final rehearsal. Don was so strong and focused, helping me figure out the song

Single and Sober: Who Found My Slipper?

I taught him. He was cool, calm, and collected as anxiety took over my confidence. Wow, I didn't expect the intense bout of fear and I had thought with doing only one song, we could do it without much stress. I took a moment to go off by myself, practice behind some trees, breathe, tune the guitar, and go sit down. All will be well. I was okay then; I could breathe again and think straight.

Funny thing, I told my sister I was singing John Denver's, "Annie's Song", so she wouldn't be suspicious if she thought I was doing a duo. The couple just prior to Don and I performed that very song. It's a good darn thing I wasn't doing that John Denver tune as I would have been furious if the person organizing the music at the reception, who had the list, let that happen. What if I didn't have another song prepared? Fortunately, it wasn't an issue, and we were ready to sing, "Leather & Lace".

The crowd went silent in anticipation. "Is love so fragile…" I started. My sister and new brother-in-law did not expect this and did not know Don could sing or that we had a song prepared for them. We took turns singing to them, then to one another on the chorus: "Lover's forever / face to face / My city or mountain / stay with me stay / I need you to love me / I need you to stay / Give to me your leather / take from me / my lace." Ooh baby ooh. Say ooh. Sing to me Don. Yes sir. We pulled it off. I think we got a standing ovation. Oh, it was so fun. The newlyweds loved it. The crowd loved it. Whew, I can breathe now. Thank you, Don and Don Henley, and of course Stevie Nicks.

My son was twenty-three years old. He walked into the reception at the park wearing a seashell bra and pink shorts. I don't even get mad, I laugh, tease, and play with him. We all took pictures with my colorful son. The bride, his aunt, told him to dress casually, and he took her literally. He bought short pink shorts and a seashell bra/top for this occasion. Only my delightful son could pull this off.

The young cousins all sat drinking in the back of the aisles of picnic tables, the musicians all took turns singing and playing in the front of the pavilion. The aunts and uncles, older cousins, friends, and extended family filled up the middle and were gracious and loving as I bopped around reacquainting myself with each one of them.

It looks like Don and I are a couple as we continuously touch base with one another before exploring the room. I felt like we were a couple. It felt nice. I'm not swimming upstream trying to make something work that I know in my gut isn't going to. This felt different, so right. We are with family and there's nothing to hide. He's my people. He's in recovery, he's in with my biological family and in with my recovery family. Don can talk about his alcoholism, and he understands me, where I've been, where I'm at, and where I'm going. This partnership does not get any better for me.

We clean up and Don takes me back to my car, well, my friend Teddy's borrowed black Trans Am that I am driving. We make plans for the next day, my last day in town. He wants to take me on a mystery date like my sister and the groom have been doing. Are you kidding? I borrowed this idea from my sister in the past and prepared a mystery date for one of the people I met online and thought it was so fun. The guy didn't appreciate it really, but I did. I'm jealous of the newlyweds with their mystery dates and now Don is doing this for me, seriously???!!! I can't wait!

Single and Sober: Who Found My Slipper?

A mystery date is when one person decides on a day and time and plans a surprise event. They only give clues as to whether to eat prior or not, and a general way to dress. I'm told to dress casually and not to eat. With butterflies in my belly, anticipation and curiosity in my mind, I'm ready early the next day when Don arrives.

He picks me up for breakfast. We went to a great restaurant followed by a tour around the Detroit River. This is where Don usually rides his bicycle. We visit his friends that run the Llama farm and visit all the Llama's he has made friends with since he began biking out on Elk Isle. He surprises me with a finale before he must get me back to Teddy's in time to pack for the airport. He takes me to the nature park to visit his other friend, the blind owl.

This doesn't exactly sound half as romantic as it was. He holds my hand for the first time and starts to talk about our future. He tells me he is Catholic, and his values are that he is married before having sex. What? Wow. Really? So unusual for a guy. Cool. Okay, we get through that. We share a few stories of romances that were close but didn't pan out.

He looks into my eyes, he holds my head with both hands, and then he kisses me. Slow, sensual, longing. Oh my. For real? A truly special first kiss. Wow. He skips while holding my hand and screams out to nature, "I Really Like you, Karen Foley!" and I return the sentiment. "I Really Like you, Don Kardashian". We grin, we laugh, we kiss again. My heart is racing. Sweeeeeet.

He gets me back to Teddy's in the nick of time. I pack, and we head off to the airport. We discussed my next trip in a month when I fly into Chicago for work. Don wants to drive down to see me then, it's only a four-hour trip.

The airport scene was like an old black and white movie playing in slow motion. We separated, truly missing one another before we even parted. We each held out our hand in the air with a still wave goodbye as I walked backward into the airport. I want to pinch myself. Is this for real? Did this really happen? Oh my God, I am beyond thrilled. I do believe I have a boyfriend. I hate to say that out loud as I've jinxed it in the past getting ahead of myself. However, I am thinking, "I have a boyfriend"!

I write in my journal the entire airplane ride across the continent. My mind is racing. What will my future hold? Could I move to MI until his parents die? Could he come and stay with me in WA? Could we actually date if I moved in with Teddy? Could I rent out my house?

I could give up my two jobs in a heartbeat. I could just stick to the one position as a National Trainer, traveling, or pick up Social Work in Detroit. I might stay put and see how the next year pans out. We could buy a cabin on the river in the Cascade mountains and fly home to MI every month or two.

The options are endless. I am so freaking excited. He's financially secure, spiritually grounded, and physically fit. He is emotionally available, bright, and mentally stable. I cannot believe the resemblance of my dream mate that I wrote about in my online dating profile under the perfect match because that is exactly who he is. The Universe is so good, loving, kind, and generous.

We text and share photos the night I arrived home. I show him the mountains from the sky where the Cascades peak through the clouds at sunset. He understands why I love the Northwest. He wants to join me. Ooh baby ooh, one day soon you will. Until then, I will see you in Chicago. Don wants to know the dates so he can get time off work. I will stay an extra day or two and spend those evenings with him. Will he get his own room? We'll figure it out. I can't wait.

The next morning, he texted me to set up a time to talk. Weird. This guy texts me all day and night. I wonder what's up. I let him know when I can be available for an actual phone call, uninterrupted.

Two days after I'm back, Don calls to say he can't do this. Huh? What are you saying? You want to break up? You are not divorced? I knew that. Oh, you are Catholic and you can't date while you are still married. Huh? I'm so confused. Are you still with her? No. Are you getting back with her? No. Are you in the court process of your divorce? Yes and No. Oh. You are continuing to work out the financial details. You agreed not to divorce before the end of the year and it's July. Tax reasons. Huh? I'm so confused. What are you talking about?

You tell me you'll come back for me someday. Huh? You want me to yell at you, to be mad. Huh? I'm still digesting what you are saying. You want me to come close and to go away. You want me to be crazy into you and you want me to be mad at you. You are waiting for me to yell at you. Ugg. This is starting to feel so toxic.

I try to sleep but I can't. I toss and turn. Time goes on, but I move from feeling stunned to feeling sad. Very sad for him, for me, and for us. Then I started to realize I felt this before. Last year, with him. I was happy, so happy, then drawn in. Scared and smart, I backed off. He wasn't available. I need to do this again. Back off. He continues to call. He wants me to yell at him, be mad. I am sad. Then it occurs to me, he likes this. He wants me to come close so he can say go away.

Now I'm mad. He's a jerk. What the hell. This is a game to him. Four years since he "split up" without ever divorcing or splitting their retirement or property. He's been a flirt. He's able to draw in women. Come close, now go away. "I don't want to split my retirement", he says. Can't blame him for that but knowing his wife put up with his shit for thirty years and now he has her on a string, unable to divorce him or get her fair share unless she plays by his rules. He wouldn't leave their house for four years after they separated. OMG, this is a very sick man.

Would you yell at me now? Yes, asshole. Goodbye. You are so mean. Do you feel better now? You hide behind your Catholic morals. I remember when you asked me what I liked the most in a partner. I told you. Your moral character. Your morals kept you from jumping on me. It was the reason you gave me to not have premarital sex.

You fed me the characteristics I was looking for. They are not your morals; they were what I told you I valued. You emotionally screwed me. It was so mean. You lied about the card you gave me when we first met, when you said you never signed your wife's name. Then in the end you admitted lying about this. You present yourself as the person you think someone wants you to be. You went to great lengths to be the person I was looking for. What kind of game are you playing? Wow. It must feel good to get the women to want you by being their knight in shining armor and you are totally unavailable. Damn. Don, you are a jerk. Ouch. Your poor wife.

UPDATE – OCTOBER 2016

One year later at my brother-in-law's funeral you are married. Your poor wives. It is times like this when I again thank my God and everyone else's Gods, Goddesses, and even my lucky stars that I am single.

19 JOHN - DECEMBER 2015

I got bored, alone during the holidays again, and went back online. Today could very well be my lucky day. I met John for coffee and oooh ooh, I like him, and he likes me. Very cool. I have learned not to count my lucky stars because as sure as I do they disappear. Nothing is permanent. Today, we had a great coffee date and there is definitely a spark. He is cute, forty-seven years old, and I am fifty-six. Guess that makes me a cougar.

I am noticing that there is a chance people are attracted to my being a social worker. I do seem to attract the guys who are drawn to the helper girlfriend type. Perhaps, just like some of my sponcee's, they want me to be their counselor. It doesn't matter since I will not take on that role. He does have some baggage like all of us. I like that he has been sober seventeen-years, and once did thirty meetings in thirty days.

He was devastated when his first & only sponsor relapsed and died. John grew up with an alcoholic father that he learned was not his biological dad. He is very angry with his mother for keeping this fact from him. John has not talked with his parents since he learned this three years ago. At that time, he also found out he had a sibling he did not know about. Turns out John lived his early years through age seven with his Grandparents in Alaska. He holds great memories, respect, and adoration for his ancestors. John seems well grounded for having a messed-up family, but then, I am not sure since I'm only beginning to get to know the part of him that he is presenting to me.

I like it that John was in two loving marriages that ended on good terms. Obviously, they were not all that loving as they would probably still be together. He explains why they didn't last. The first was a woman who fell in love with another woman and their marriage ended after nine years. They are still friends. This makes sense to me and the fact they are still friends is a plus.

His second wife he made the big commitment with was a social worker that was four years older than him. They were together for eleven years and divorced two years ago. John mentions he went camping with her last summer. It sounds like he still loves her, but he notes, "she was a free spirit and never meant to settle down". The way he told it, she had affairs and he divorced her. I am curious to find out if that is her side of the story, too.

What I do not know about is if he is a dry drunk or a bum or why he is sitting on his laurels. His work history sounds stable, but I am not sure he is currently functioning like a productive member of society. He seems to have a stable background, spent three years in the Navy, four years in the reserves, and says he has military insurance. Then he worked twenty-five years in a steel factory, until a year ago when he was injured and lost part of his sight in one eye. The business he worked for was sold, and he lost all of his benefits, and would not work for the new owner.

Then his friend of twenty years, a female alcoholic, killed herself. John has been in counseling and healing this past year. He told me he is buying storage units and does not have a real job. He drives a nice-looking older Ford pickup with a canopy that's in good shape. He says he's going to sell some weed whackers after our coffee date.

It sounds like he is depressed, understandably so without his sight, his friend, parents, or a program. I do not think he left a tip at Starbucks. He seemed invested in my contributing .29 cents change, toward our beverages, rather than break the extra dollar bill. Perhaps he is not stable financially, I'm not sure. He bought the beverages. His boots were in rough shape. I was just noticing, not ruling him out. All in all, I do like him. A perfectly imperfect human I am attracted to.

I like his personality and playfulness. I am not looking for a guy to support me, but if he could support himself, I would find him much more desirable. I also would have to know he is not depressed and unmedicated, I could not deal with that. I am not even sure I could deal with someone sober without a program, though he claims he is 'spiritual' and that could be just fine. I hope he has some compass to guide his thoughts and actions. I find it attractive that he's in counseling and that he referred to 'taking accountability' when talking about his more recent marriage. He was not just blaming her, which was refreshing.

I decided to proceed, but to take it slow, and I'm certain he wants to, also. He did refer to wanting to get to know someone and I let him know we shared this desire. I

Single and Sober: Who Found My Slipper?

am so skeptical given my negative online and other dating experiences. John has trust issues given his last relationship's infidelity. I am feeling positive about this so far. I want to jump up and clap my heels, but I am much too cautious to go there, just yet.

Let's see if he lives in a tent, watch to see if his ego is right sized, and if he has some sort of program for self-reflection. I am excited, though, to have someone cool to start to get to know. I am kind of lonely these days and it will be fun to explore this possible long-term relationship. I love the idea of creating a friendship.

There could be sweet icing on the cake if he can help me change light bulbs in the dark or take down my outdoor Christmas lights from a decade ago. If he could one day help me sort through my garage, I could be forever indebted, again, not a prerequisite, just a delightful thought. John, could you be my friend, my lover, and my handyman? More will be revealed.

A few days later I went out with John again. He was quite kind, and I did see more into his character. On one hand he is at a tough time in his life, perhaps depressed; he doesn't have a real job, and he lacks self-esteem for sure. On the other hand, he has a spirit about him that is simply fun. He is a jokester, he is very present, complimentary, and a gentleman. He has a curiosity about him to know more about yoga. John is fascinated by how Yogi somebody or other was able to say his good-byes and then be so in tuned to his body that this Yogi could stop his heart when it was time to die. John is also very open minded about people who are different from him; GLBTQ, nudists, people who are in recovery, etc., and he is a liberal. My kind of man. I do like him.

Yet, I do not want to fall for his potential. Lord knows I have done that enough in my younger years. I always saw the person they could become, but they didn't always see it themselves.

I need to recognize that his dirty hands, dirty boots, and old t-shirts are how he presents. He buys storage units and goes through junk all day, looking for the needle in the haystack or other treasures. I cannot pretend this is the man who worked twenty-five years at the same steel industry because he has changed since then. I need not seek perfection; however, I do not want to end up with someone too depressed to function. I prefer someone with a real job who washes their hands and can afford new boots. Since I like his personality, I will give it a go, but I plan to take it slow.

I think four or five times I heard him say, "I suck at this" referring to this dating thing, yet his actions were admirable. He did everything right, setting up both dates, buying my appetizers and movie ticket. I offered to buy refreshments and he was not expecting it. He asked before kissing me goodnight and he was generous with heartfelt compliments. He called me smart, attractive, and then blew it by saying he doesn't feel like he is in my league.

What? He's probably thinking through the perspective that "I'm a high school graduate who's jobless and she has a master's degree and a career" like our profiles point toward. I could look at it that way too, but I am more concerned that he's not prejudiced, that he's respectful, and that he's kind. It doesn't hurt that he's liberal.

I finally feel worthy enough to be anyone's date, let alone a man nine years younger than me. I would not enjoy taking care of him financially and I am not interested in being a sad old cougar buying her a boy toy. As a woman that is an overachiever, I feel equal to a man who just gets by. I would prefer a handsome man who dresses sharp, is motivated and an achiever. I, too, have such low self-esteem that I don't feel like I am in that kind of man's league. I need to work on believing I do deserve to have a decent, productive partner, and not pick guys that need saving.

My tendency is to focus on that part of John who is spiritually curious and who wants to not just complain about the size of his gut but focus' instead on the part of him that wants to do something about it. I'm not sure he has moved from precontemplation to contemplation in that stage of change, though, as Miller and Rollnick would point out. They are the masters of Motivational Interviewing. John doesn't eat healthy, he despises exercise, and he is not interested in changing as he grieves his old life and that of his friend who died by suicide.

John has good taste in women. He says he hasn't drunk alcohol or used drugs in seventeen years. He could be interested in at least attending speaker's meetings, and he would fit in with my sick friends, possibly even my family too. He is down to earth and pleasant to be with. He is open-minded and liberal; I really like that. What you see is what you get.

When John talks about his ex-wife who left him for a woman, he doesn't hate all lesbians, and he doesn't hate her. He responds with words and body language of how hard that was initially, but how they are still friends. How cool is that? His second wife he separated from two years ago and they are still friends, too. I like this. The only major flaw I see is his depression. I cannot let my sick co-dependent type tendencies start this relationship by trying to fix him. He is who he is. I am not responsible for his mental wellness or recovery.

All in all, I believe I am drawn to a part of him that I would like to explore. Is he at all interested in going down a recovery path with me? I do believe he is. I like that he is scared, I usually am, too. I will be when the kissing goes further, and he wants to come to my house. For now, I have gotten quite good at this dating scene, if it is not too intimate immediately. I need it to move forward slowly and naturally, and I will be fine.

He sent his morning text. I told him, "Thanks for another great date. I like you".

John and I texted for another day and then I got a text from him that caught me off guard. There he is at 1:30 in the afternoon texting me a selfie from his bed. He is shirtless and I'm looking at a big round dark ball of hair. Gross, not pretty. He has a nice face, but his hairy body is not attractive, nor is his half naked waist up picture. Let's not even talk about being in bed at 1:30 in the afternoon.

Weird. I can't respond. I am starting to question if I am a lesbian since I am not attracted to him. Then I remind myself of all the men I do find attractive and the cells in my body start to react. If I don't like round hairy bodies, it does not mean I don't like men or that I must like women. Breathe. I could love his body if I loved him. It is just weird. I am thinking, shave and put your shirt back on. I do not know how to respond. I want to be kind. Open-minded and kind.

I sleep on it. The next day I looked at the photo and knew I could be with him if I was in love. The shock was not expecting that picture and never even considering what he would look like naked. Who am I to judge? I am old and have a gut, I have scars and wrinkles, dry skin and I know this skin-deep thing is temporary. If I grew to love him, I would love that hairy body, too. This is silly and I'm overreacting.

I texted him in the morning: Heeey. Your picture took me off guard. I wasn't ready to see you in bed yet, lol. How are you doing today? We get back to chatting throughout the rest of the day. The next day, too. We are back on track, cool.

John tells me about how cold he is, but he likes sleeping when he can see his breath. I am thinking we could have problems in the future sleeping together as I need a heated mattress pad, a space heater, and a heated blanket when it gets below fifty degrees.

Then he shocks me again with a text of how he hates living with his wife. WTF really? I responded. He hates living with her husband and her mother. I am so confused, and I know at that moment what we have been building that hasn't really started is already over.

It took me a minute to realize that his text actually said his "x wife". He hates living with his "x wife" and her husband and her mother. Drama. Duh. They must really hate living with you, too, I thought. Since he divorced two years ago and he did answer my prior question about how he was 'self-sufficient', I wasn't expecting that to mean he divorced but never moved out of his wife's house. It doesn't matter if I am jumping to conclusions. I do not want to be with someone who lives with his ex. It is becoming a theme. I wonder what percentages of men that do online dating are 'living with their ex's'. Maybe he is divorced, but he has not moved on.

He continued to contact me that night and the next day. I do the right thing by sending the following text: "I like you, John, but I'm not interested in pursuing this because of the dynamics of your living situation. Thanks for showing me a good time. Good luck in your future." He responds, "I'm very sorry to hear that, but I totally understand. You're a wonderful woman".

I can't make this stuff up. It's my life and I'm sticking to it.

Why am I still hopeful I will find "the one"? I am a diehard victim of the Cinderella fairy tale such that I know it's fiction, yet I continue to seek it like a desperate, horny Hogwart. Are Hogwarts desperate? Are they horny? I don't know.

I don't know why my life seems incomplete without a partner; I only know it's what I seek to ad nauseam. I'm unsure if I should continue to chase the dream or accept the reality of swimming upstream.

even the rich white guys who can afford to be on the Event focused sites are starting to look attractive to me. However, the concept of buying an elite partner repulses me. Simultaneously, it intrigues me. It goes against every grain of moral fiber I have and yet, it could work to my benefit. It's a racist, classist overt practice that a part of me wants in on. My sister and her husband met through their singles camp social club. Would she have paid $2,000 for him? Undoubtedly yes. My sponsee and the love of her life paid that much to meet each other. On top of that they paid for the event fee to go underwater diving or snorkeling or something like that. They have never regretted it. Hmm. I contemplate the pros and cons.

As tired as I have been, I agreed to go to an interview with the owner of In The Loop, an events-based club on the Uppity Eastside of Seattle, the newer version of Events and Adventurers. Knowing all along I might have to have a scene in their office about how wrong this is. I get dressed to the hilt and drive there with both hope and fury.

I attempt to dart to the Eastside after work in rush hour only to find the freeway is a parking lot. Excited, nervous, creating both the story of finding true meaningful romance with someone who can pay their own way and afford to take me out, along with the story that all this is nonsense and I need to picket their office.

Who knows? Maybe I could meet someone who could take me on a trip to Europe or Africa. Maybe love and marriage. I do not want to give up on the Cinderella story even though I know it's a lie. I still want Prince Charming to sweep me off my feet and carry me to safety from this harsh, cruel world. I want someone to protect me. I am not a damsel in distress though. I am just a Damsel.

Maybe. A Dame? I would choose a better word. Not a desperate housewife. No one should marry a house. Am I desperate or dazzling? Am I a lonely lunatic driving to the Eastside or a down to earth real woman looking to buy a real man that I don't have to support? How much for that dude? She asks as she combs through the album of available rich white men tossing her long hair behind her shoulder.

Then I laugh at how stupid and vulnerable I've been waiting for the Disney version of my life that simply never comes. I wonder why I think I need a partner to make my life complete. Why can't I simply appreciate all that I have? I have such a freaking wonderful life. I have enough! Enough money, love, dating, family, clothes, comfy house, brand new car, yadda yadda yadda. I have more than enough and then some. I'm spoiled, I have my spirit, my health, awareness, a great job, a wonderful healthy son, a super dog. I have stillness I learned from practicing meditation and I'm part of a spiritual community. I have so much love. Why, oh why, do I continue to seek happiness outside of myself?

I am vulnerable when I walk into the office of In The Loop. I remember that interview fifteen years ago. I was so ready to buy in, using my income tax return to make it happen. I was drawn into the events and the more natural way of gathering with other singles doing fun stuff. The $300 I planned to spend, even the $500 I had, was not enough. They wanted $2,000. At the time I thought, no freakin' way. I will not buy my spouse. I won't be bought. No way in hell.

Now it is fifteen years later, I'm fifty-six and feeling more desperate and anxious to spend the rest of my life with someone. I despise the rude method of online dating. These sites send me so many faces to pick from every day. I am expected to look at a face and decide yes or no. Interested or not. Swipe right or swipe left, you don't even read their profile. I can buy up and get the 'privilege' of knowing when and if they read my email. Knowing that any person to whom I send an email could be stalking me and deciding what it means if I read their email, if I don't respond right away, or if I don't read their email. I don't want a stalker. I don't want to decide yes or no based only on a photo. I don't want to go through 300 more coffee dates. I'm starting to think single social events are not such a bad idea. I go into the building. I am thinking it's the same building I went to back in 2001 or so.

Now I am more prepared. I know what they are going to try to sell me. I make good money now, $2,000 is worth considering, though I tell myself no matter what I am going to sleep on it. If the heavy sales pitch does not allow one to sleep on the investment, the answer will be no.

The office is not the same as last time. It is a simple three-room office. The owner is behind the closed door and the young receptionist is quite chatty. She is from my small town and is amazed that I drove in traffic to come all the way to Bellevue in rush hour. She is quick to show me the recent calendars of events. She told me about their trip last month to Ireland and I was an instant shoe-in. I could see myself doing an overseas trip. Ireland would have been a blast. They are planning to go to Whistler in the Winter and Australia next year, both of which I would go to in a heartbeat. How fun, I'm liking this already.

The whole feel is different than before; no catalogs

of men in fake poses in four different outfits: business, casual, in nature and whatever. I wasn't asked to bring changes of clothes for photos, or to pay for a professional photographer and profile. I am shown just a calendar full of small and large group activities separated by age groups and different levels of physical activity. These are all things I appreciate.

The owner, Susan, was 5 '11", vivacious, and started her business as any good rebel would do after working for Events and Adventures. She found there wasn't enough consideration put into, for example, assuring tall men would be at events. Susan had no intention to go out with men shorter than her. She worked for the original company and became the head of East Coast Sales by linking people that desired to be together. She continually referred to her events that put the forties/fifties and sixties in separate events from the twenties and thirties, a woman after my own heart. I loved her spunk, energy, and detail orientation. I wanted to sign the dotted line just to support her rebel attitude toward the mother agency. She talked proudly about how she made them a lot of money and how now she's going to make herself a lot of money. I loved her.

At the same time, I know I'm being sold, and she is very good at this. The questions were personal, and I drew my boundary when she asked, "Do you keep at least a thousand dollars in your bank account?" to which I answered that "it is none of your business". She then said she just wanted to make sure I could pay my bills and I wasn't looking for a sugar daddy. All the people she accepts are self-sufficient. Smooth. I still wouldn't answer, and she moved on.

Single and Sober: Who Found My Slipper?

She did hesitate one second when I told her I liked her, I liked what she created in her business, and I would need to sleep on it when she made me the final offer of $2,000 spread over eighteen months for a membership that goes on as long. I left feeling confident I would join, but I would do it knowingly and willingly with consciousness. As I pulled out of the parking lot I'm thinking, I'm going to buy me a spouse, ha-ha, knowing full well it goes against every moral fiber I am built on. I've been Cinderella my whole life and now I'm going to find my Prince Charming darn it. I've got the job, the house, the dog. It's time for a man with $1,000+ in his checking account too.

I went out to eat and while pigging out on lasagna style chocolate caramel dessert after eating half my eggplant parmesan, I started checking out the better business bureau. The name brings up a different singles group at the same location with nine complaints and nine resolved complaints bringing it to an "A" standard. I read the complaints, and they are either about the heavy sales tactics and not being able to get out of the contract or about lame events. I started to think about all the speed dating events and the Valentine's Day singles groups from my past. I remember when seven women in my age group showed up and only one man came for the fifties age group. Hmm. That could happen for sure. Let me think about this. I have learned these social events bring out the women, but we are often outnumbered compared to the men. The younger crowd outnumbers the older singles every time, also.

I talked to my sister to see if she paid to go on those singles camp outs where she met her husband. Sure, but not too much more than normal camping costs. The social club was built by natural desires to continue communicating with these folks after camp. She isn't sure if she would have paid dues and membership fees or if she would have gone to events a few times a month or more. My sister does suggest I talk to members who do frequent the events and get their take, even though that may be biased picked recipients if I request references. I will ask though.

Just then I got another invite from a different meet-up singles group about a party that is happening on Saturday. How wonderful. I will go to the mixer and see how it feels. I am so tired I have no business going out, but I force myself to follow through as an experiment. I wanted to see if I was "booked" to go out three times a month for the next eighteen months to Bellevue or Seattle based events, if I would actually have the energy to do it. Because if I didn't go, I wouldn't go normally. If I wouldn't go normally, well there's eighteen months of payments and $2,000 down the drain. I planned to go out on Saturday as a test of my commitment to myself in being adventurous and energized enough to attend even one event that has no money or commitment attached.

Saturday night came and I put on my courageous front despite a sprained ankle and a lot of fear. I got in my car and headed to the east side. After being perplexed when I arrived at the gigantic parking garage basement, I reminded myself to breathe. I was at level P3 and reading that the Billiards & Bar I sought was on level three. I could not grasp where the heck level three was if it wasn't on the floor where I stood, but this was just a parking garage. Eventually, security pointed me up to the 3rd level above ground using a different elevator. Duh.

I Stepped out of the elevator to find the fanciest pool hall in all of WA. It wasn't the dive pool hall I was used to, nor did I really expect that in uptown Bellevue. Being lost and confused, walking around on my sprained ankle, being scared to go to this event, all made the possibility that I turn around and run home seem inviting.

However, I am glad I stayed. Even though I was probably the second oldest in the room, I felt thirty-five and laughed lightheartedly as if I belonged.

Rita has been hosting mixers for a long time and she is very good at running her singles events. I'd been to four or five of her hosted dating events. This mixer was an all-age group event with one hundred people invited, of whom about sixty-five showed up. Half her audience were young gay men, which was very cool as I like a socially accepting mixed crowd. Some were married folks who came back to share their stories of having met at Rita's prior events. One couple was engaged during this fundraiser mixer that benefitted colon cancer research.

The bingo game as an icebreaker suited me well because it brought out my silly and competitive side. After a few awkward interviews with the boys, I got into the spirit and asked lots of men lots of personal questions, and I had a very good time. I connected with several guys, most of whom were my son's age, gay, or both. There were a couple of men who were probably closer to my age, like in their forties (I'm in my fifties). I played the thumb war game and lost. I created a new best friend handshake. I also quoted my favorite lyrics from Jackson Browne to a guy who wrote down this ancient musician's name to look him up later. Jackson Browne's Pretender lyrics were perfect for the moment. "Caught between the longing for love / And the struggle for the legal tender / ...Are you there? Say a prayer / For the Pretender / Who started out so young and strong / Only to surrender". It was a sweet night all in all.

I was confident in my social skills and that increased as I got more comfortable. It wasn't until the end when I challenged myself to spend another five dollars on a diet coke and stick around as people were pairing up that I was uncomfortable again. Awkward to be the one left standing holding a full coke with a thick ass straw. I cannot believe bartenders don't have a clue about that. It's like wearing a sash that says I'm a drunk, don't give me liquor! Combine that with being the last one standing and we are not referring to the funniest comedian who gets the gig. It was another moment when I knew it was time to go home, oh hurry quick. I gave myself permission to run out, barely having drank a sip or two of my drink and trying not to limp with my swollen ankle so sore I could barely walk.

After all was said and done, I was glad that I went. I could see I would be sociable and have fun at the Bellevue singles club if I decided to join. I could even meet friends, who knows, maybe even a partner. But the reality that it took every ounce of energy within me to go to Bellevue was significant. I would not want to travel there or to Seattle once a week or three times a month only to find myself the last one standing. The fifty-six-year-old pathetic single woman without a life. It feels embarrassing. At least with online dating I stick to my neighborhood. I go out with someone I get an imaginary spark from. I meet on my schedule. Not on an events schedule where the fifty-sixties age group meet early on Wednesday afternoon, like we are all retired. No, I could regret spending $2,000 and agreeing to do that regularly. Now & again, sure, but use it or lose two grand, no way.

I settled for $20 a month to join a new dating site, Match.com. I have an old friend who recently met his current girlfriend there, and it seems a more sensible site than Plenty of Fish, for sure. My OurTime subscription expired and plenty of fish is free but not worth the price. One can meet pigs on the fishy site. Cat phishing animals. Then there's me, the Princess looking for Prince Charming in a sea of kitties and pigs. Geez, one day I will get it right. I do not really think of myself as a Princess or certainly not as all that, but when I meet some of the prospects on Plenty of Fish, I am convinced I am not all that bad either.

It is strange that as I get deeper into the Buddhist Recovery Practice, I should find myself seeking something outside myself to make me feel good inside. I am starting to know too much to believe this is even a possibility.

My greatest fear is rejection. My experience so far has been that these sites are full of both getting rejected and rejecting others. I hate both. If it takes 300 fishies to find the fish you want to keep, does that mean 299 fishies are being thrown back into the sea? Rejected? Alone. That is just sickening. It has been said that with online dating it seems the odds are good to meet the boys, but the goods are odd, as is the game.

I am going to bed now. Hopefully simply with gratitude for all I have. My higher power, my son, my dog, my family, my friends, my house, and my small yard filled with poop, weeds, flowers and trees. I love my life. It is complete. The rest is entertainment. Yee-ha.

21 COACH GARY – MAY 2016

Recently I've gone out with two guys from Match.com and flirted with a guy at church. First was Coach Gary, who seemed a little odd on the dating site, but it was hard to tell if online communicating wasn't his thing. I gave him the benefit of the doubt as my generation is not so savvy with online tasks which could account for the oddness. Gary works at Boeing and at first, I thought he liked to coach kids' sports, but it wasn't clear. I agreed to meet him at a park after I returned from my upcoming trip. I learned he was a life coach. I immediately went into judgment mode as I'm a trained therapist and get mad at people making money without a license and have no real training or regulation to oversee the quacks playing counselors under a different name. However, I do appreciate the whole concept of peer-based teaching, so I try to keep an open mind.

I was exhausted as I got in from my work trip to IA in the middle of the night. I woke up about 9:00 am after half a night's sleep, confused and in a different time zone. I decided after some quick food that I needed to sleep all day. I didn't bother to check my calendar or set my alarm.

I was embarrassed because I totally forgot I had a date to meet in a park at noon the next day with Coach Gary. At noon he texted me "are you here"? Since I knew he had come from Camano Island, quite a distance, I felt terrible standing him up. I let him know I got in late; I could be there in thirty minutes. He chose to wait rather than reschedule and I high tailed it out the door, not prepared for a date; no shower, minimal makeup, barely dressed. It was okay, though, as it was a date on a eighty-degree Spring Day at the Stillaguamish River up north in Arlington. I managed to show up, which was amazing given the circumstances.

I knew at once that Coach Gary was probably Autistic. He was a kind man, very timid and shy, and enthused about only one thing: Life Coaching. He'd been empowered through a lady at work who was charging him money to have sessions with him and who helped him recognize what he wanted in his life. When Gary found his voice, he was able to give his wife the divorce she asked for, but he learned he could ask for what he wanted with his Grandkids. He had never spoken up before for anything. He raised his wife's son for twenty-five years but was never considered Grandpa to the kids. He was Gary to his Stepson and Gary to the Grandkids and he spent no time with either. Now that he and his wife divorced, he became Grandpa, he found his voice, and his entire life changed.

I was glad to see him light up at the empowerment process that his life coach helped him to find. It was fun to see him resonate at helping others, too, and to know he's now taken on life coaching with someone else at Boeing. I could not imagine him coaching another, though. His speech was very slow, and his confidence barely above ground level. I found him rather annoying, as dear as he was. His thick glasses, the stuttering, the simpleness. I thought he had a kind soul, but I was not attracted. Gary worked with his coach to realize his latest goal of online dating and next he was going to remodel his house. I could tell he was becoming the best version of himself he had ever known.

We had a sweet date, but I knew at once he wasn't for me. I talked about my work on the crisis line, and I think he was interested, even though he may have at one time been a client. He seemed more functional than many people I've worked with. He probably thought I was a conceded flake which is what I felt like after leaving him waiting so long then being quick to send the "I didn't really feel a spark and I'm guessing you didn't either" email. We wished each other well.

22 BILL – MAY 2016

Next was Bill. Right off the get go on his first email he asked, "Would you be open to meeting over dinner for a conversation some evening?" I normally would not be open to someone being so bold as to leave out the hello, I'm Bill- chit chat but I've come to realize that what I imagine usually is not true anyway. Bill seemed like a nice guy on paper and the chit chat doesn't compare to one-on-one time anyway, so what the heck. I said yes.

We set up a date at a nice restaurant over the weekend and tried to back track on the chit chat and that was awkward. Bill was older than I was seeking, but he was only out of my range by a year, and he was only ten years older than myself. Between his picture and his profile, he seemed active and fit so I was hoping he could inspire me as I've fallen off my health plan over the past couple years.

When I arrived at the restaurant I knew at once that Bill was too old for me. I shouldn't have worn the cute fedora hat I grabbed at the last second to keep my hair dry in this Seattle rain. Bill was too old to appreciate my young spirit of risk-taking costumes. Looking across the table all

I see are warts and wrinkles. I want to be kind, I want to be attracted, but I am not. At all.

Bill started to lecture me when I ordered a diet soda and I began to get an attitude. Really? I am tired. I know soda is not good for me and I am choosing it anyway, lay off buddy. But I am kind and go along with him, yeah yeah yeah. I know I know I know. I am off track with my health plan. Now, can we order and get this over with?

When I think about these things, I know I send that energy into the room. I can wear a smile and send daggers. I do my best to be present and engage. Naturally, I will not say a thing about being in recovery or getting his reaction that I love hanging out with recovering alcoholics and drug addicts. I have learned to withhold that information until the third date at least, and most encounters do not make it that far.

Bill is retired and enjoying it. I started to talk about work, and he changed the subject. No big deal, I don't really want to talk about the crisis line anyway. I mentioned I was on call and would apologize ahead of time if I got a call that I would have to take. It wouldn't mean I would have to leave, but I would have to answer the phone. Bill thought my statement was strange, like why would he care if I took a call? I found it odd to question my kind intentions of informing him in advance that it wouldn't be personal if I interrupted our date to take a call.

Bill told me about his grandkids and his garden. I started to tell him about my own business where I get to travel and be a consultant and speaker for 'human service professionals', again leaving out the details about working with clients facing domestic violence, drug addiction, and homelessness, but once again he changed the subject. This time not as smoothly, saying he's retired and does not want to talk about work.

Well okay then. We ate. He complained about the food at the restaurant I'd chosen. After dinner he walked me to my car and made a crack about, "Oh you're in this fancy car" and I knew beyond a doubt this was not a man I wanted to ever see again. There is nothing wrong with owning a car that isn't a clunker, one that breaks down every month or more.

I still could not get over that he was so old. Nooooo. I hate it that he's even within a decade of me. It is so hard to believe that I was dating someone my dad's age, or so it seemed. Aging is an odd thing especially when I still feel so young and have an abundance of love to share.

My therapist told me a couple days later that I need to be looking closer to the young fifty year old range rather than the sixty-five end of the spectrum. I got online again and changed my preferences to seek a man from forty-five to sixty rather than forty-nine to sixty-five. What the hell. I am grossed out by most of the sixty-year old's. I suppose I'm an ageist. There is a big difference between men who are fifty and those in their sixties. I can grow into being old, no doubt, with anyone. Starting out with a retiree is not quite what I'm prepared for at this time.

I wonder if being checked out on drugs for seventeen years makes me think I'm seventeen years younger than my current age. That would make me thirty-nine. Yes, I think that is it. I am a thirty-nine-year-old in a fifty-six-year-old body. I am in my prime. Then again, I started using in my teens so that makes me a teenager emotionally, give or take my sober time. Either way, these freaking old guys are not right for me and my thinking is distorted. Maybe if I had grown old with them it would be fine. Baby bald without wrinkles and with kind eyes would be okay. Gosh, I am so judgmental. Surface level judgment. It's rude and wrong and true. I don't feel like I'm that picky, but I can't see myself with someone from a totally different era.

23 MICHAEL – MAY 2016

I am excited to report that today I noticed a guy at the Unity church that I hadn't seen before. He appeared to be alone, he was very attractive, and I'm guessing between forty-five and fifty years old. He had big brown eyes and a great smile, and we were checking each other out. I attended the after-service coffee klatch. When I went to sit in my usual seat it was taken and so were the seats at the entire table. I spotted a seat on the loveseat available and realized he was sitting right next to it in the chair. At first, I got nervous and headed toward the door, a silly move since my hands were filled with snacks and it was obvious I was looking for a seat, not to leave. I boldly and proudly said, Mind if I sit here? to which he pointed as I caught him with his mouth full.

I sat down and we looked into each other's eyes. It was such a great moment. I had just meditated like Kate the speaker told us to do. "Imagine something you want in your life, really see it". There I was visualizing the perfect relationship. Barbequing in my backyard. Doing it. Seeing it. And now, here he is. Seconds later. Manifested. God is so good. I am living in heaven on earth.

He started the conversation describing how hard it was to meditate since his head injury. "Even before the accident I had ADHD, now trying to meditate, I can't do it. I start out following the directions and then I can't hear. I can't even hear anymore. I think I need a hearing aid", he said in a confused state.

Michael is his name. I am unclear if his eyes are rolling back in his head. When he speaks to me, is his hard-working brain trying to find the right words or if there is an entire disconnect because of the brain injury? In any case I'm trying to keep an open mind.

Quit ruling out every guy you meet, Karen. Here's a guy you thought was cute 5 minutes ago, and sent from God, and just because he can't form sentences or keep a thought straight doesn't mean he's not a great guy. I acknowledged his difficulty with meditation and asked him when and how his brain injury occurred. "1999 going eighty-five I hit a wall in my car I'm told", he continues, "you would not believe how far I've come". He went on to explain how he wasn't expected to function at all.

I sometimes wonder if I'm not looking for an equal partner as that would scare me. Taking on someone like this as a project where I could feel good about helping is what I'm drawn toward. That would be less intimidating than being with the grown-up gorgeous GQ man walking by me at that moment, dressed in an ironed purple shirt and khakis, with a sweater tied over his shoulder. So dreamy.

I envision Michael loving me like no other man could and the GQ dude being all bossy and controlling. These are the types of lies and made-up stories that go through my mind. The GQ dude gets his wife, and they leave together; the perfect looking church couple. I'm so tainted by my work I think, yeah, they look good here, but what goes on behind closed doors?

Michael returns after getting a snack and explains how he wants to come check me out at the Buddhist Recovery meeting tonight at the same church. Only he's not sure he can come because he is the sole caretaker of his mother with Alzheimer's. I let him know it was a drop-in group, to come whenever he could. He reminded me that he would come to check me out. Cute. It is obvious he has a broken brain, no filter. I am so drawn to this type of raw honesty. I find newcomers at every meeting and have these very similar conversations. I need a new pool of men to draw from.

Michael never showed up to the Buddhist Recovery group I was facilitating later that night at the church. He didn't show up at future meetings either. I would have liked to get to know him better.

24 TO DATE OR NOT TO DATE – MAY 2016

I don't think it is fair for me to be online dating. How could I possibly be available to love or care for another? I am busy, my cup is full, and I've been single for so long I would have a hard time adjusting to having a partner. Yet, I long for intimacy. I am willing to appreciate another and work together to create a life for this last phase of doing the real deal. But could I really? It has been twenty-four years since I have been in a significant relationship. No boyfriend for decades! Why? Sober and Single. It cannot be for lack of trying. Should I persevere or let it go?

Do I rule everyone out? Could this be decades of bad luck? Or is it good luck? I listen to my married friends and patients and so much energy is spent wishing their partners would act differently. I also know beyond a doubt from the information I had to reason with at the time, I have not passed up someone that I later regretted turning away. I must admit, though, that I may be quick to rule out some guys before really getting to know them, and I'm sure others have done the same to me.

I think God has something wonderful in store. I am not sure if I should be thanking my lucky stars right here and right now that I do not have a mate to obsess about, blame, and worry over. I don't have a partner to be the excuse for my misery or my joy. Should I be hanging onto one last very thin thread of hope that God has that perfectly healthy recovering person who loves meditation and is wise, creative, and kind in store for me? That special someone who pulls his weight that I can adore who is just around the corner if only I just keep looking.

I am about to give up on this fairy tale. I could be in heaven right here, right now. Enjoying life without stressing over a relationship.

Then, I got this message at church. Visualize. Manifest.

I pray for God's will and maybe, just maybe, this is it. I have a great life. I have a great home that I can afford. I have a terrific son, a fabulous dog and two out of four living siblings. I have the greatest of friends and family. I have a demanding, but well-paying job, where I get to be the boss.

The cool thing is that I do not have to do the supervisory duties I don't enjoy. For instance, it's not my job to have to fire people or produce grueling monthly reports. Instead, I get to be a clinical supervisor; I get to give input and sometimes great ideas. Occasionally, my ideas are even implemented at work by the management, something that never happened when I was front line staff.

In addition, I get to be my own boss in my side business. It's fun to travel and be known as the trainer, the advocate, the counselor, the expert, especially when I get paid big bucks to do what I love. Safety and sobriety, throw in sanity as I learn more about mental illness and my specialty becomes Triple Play.

Triple Play Connections is my third job, a not-for-profit I started and have operated for a decade. Training advocates that work with survivors to help them get stable, somewhat sober, and away from their perpetrators; that's one of my missions in life.

Do I even have time for a partner? I would probably continually let them down because I do not cook much, I do not even walk my dog often, I do not mow, or spend much down time at home. Really, I am living the dream, and this could be God's will.

This is happiness Karen style.

Why do I feel so empty when I spend day after day without intimacy? Thank God for my meetings and the intense, in-depth, real, raw emotions that fill my cup. Spirit is using me. I am a vehicle for others at work, at meetings, on the road, in Triple Play Connections, and in 12-Step business meetings. As Rickey Beyers sings, "Use me / ohh God". She is so good. Rickey could make an atheist become a believer. I feel the love. Love is all there is.

I am grateful and sometimes lonely. I am full and sometimes empty. At times I want to fill my soul hole. I am ego and sometimes I'm in Unity. It is all good. My feelings pass as they are impermanent, and this too shall pass. Good passes. Joy passes. Death passes. I am okay with dying. I am afraid of pain. Pain of grief, sickness, rejection, and not feeling good enough. It all passes. I begin to notice and not cling to my thoughts or beliefs. I let go of attachment and expectations. I join the next online dating site and let God do the rest.

Single and Sober: Who Found My Slipper?

I need to give myself the same advice that I give my friend Teddy who can't seem to quit drinking. If you want it, there is hope. Surrender and get out of the way. Let the miracle happen. This could be my "love life". I surrender and let God lead the way. Now, I need to get out of the way and let the miracle happen. If this is the miracle, then thank you God for my idols who gave me schoolgirl giggles and my soulmate who sang with me in harmony and those lovers I have known who "Tried hard to help me / You know put me at ease / And loved me so naughty / Made me weak in the knees " as Joni Mitchell would sing in "River".

25 THINKING BACK – SUMMER 2016

Prior to sobriety, I had many special relationships. My first date at sixteen years old was with my forever love who wrote me poems in his rich handwriting with the wisdom of an elder and who forever holds my heart. Through him I learned I have so much love to give.

The seventies were a time of experimenting with sex, drugs, and rock-n-roll. I had fun. It was a different time. I took chances. I am so blessed to be able to hitch-hike around Ann Arbor, MI, hang out with strangers, try acid, cocaine, and reefer, bad boys and good boys, and live to tell about it, mostly unscathed.

My artist friend who made my heart tick was the coolest man I had ever met on this earth. My love life has not been without knowing lust and love. I was not afraid to give love and get love. It has just been more than a while now.

I think I am a born-again virgin. I am not going to bars or hanging out with the drug crowd. If that was all the love in store for me, I am happy I have known love, multiple times, in multiple ways. I do know what love is. So do many of the men I have been with.

Then there was my Irish friend and lover from the eighties. He was a fun and exciting guy. A great dart player, a semi-regular at the bar where I worked, who drove a topless Jeep and owned a home. He had been married and then divorced with two kids. He invited me over to his home for a BBQ and invited his mother to our first date. I loved that he was a mama's boy, but I wasn't impressed with being judged.

As a bartender, both he and his mom had their doubts about me. Still, we became dart and drinking buddies and had a great time getting to know one another. I left on vacation for a week, and I told my family I found the man I was going to marry. He got back with an ex-girlfriend after dropping me off at the airport. At least he had the decency to tell me where he stood when he picked me up at the airport. We spent one evening saying good-bye, letting me be mad and get over it.

Love is all there is. I have known a lot of love in these past twenty-four years in recovery. Not only the kind like I just described, but intimate love with God, with my son, through 12-Step meetings, through family, through recovering addicts and alcoholics, at work, and with sponsor's and sponsee's. My life is filled with love, filled with God, filled with random acts of kindness.

I do not understand how I can be so full, so happy, so loved one moment and completely forgetful the next. I start to believe that the pain is too great or that I will somehow die if I don't get that next fix, that next sugar rush, some shopping adrenaline, or that next caffeine buzz.

Then I feel horrible about showing up to my employee's memorial all cranked out on caffeine. Or I start to hide behind the omission of the gambling problem until the lie takes me back to the casino. I am convinced having a feeling is going to kill me that I take the reins and self-sabotage. This disease is insane.

Thank-you God. Tonight, I told on myself at the Buddhist Recovery Group. Honesty is the one spiritual principle I practice that saves me. I saw that my big secret was ready to kill me. I quit last October for the third time, no more gambling. I meant it. Only there I was doing the same thing and expecting a different result. Tonight, in telling the truth I knew it could not come at a better time. Twenty-four years clean and I am drowning. I need to trust God, be honest with my Sangha, my spiritual community. I need to let the miracle work in my life. No more gambling, I am done. Feel the grief, accept it, move on being kind to myself and others.

I sent out another half dozen messages on Match.com earlier today. If this is God's will, I am certainly putting myself out there. Something is telling me that this is not God's will. It could be twenty-four years of trying and barely having a second date. Perhaps God's will is clear through all the love that surrounds me that I am free to spend time with the newcomer and not have to rush home to cook dinner or eat with my mate. I am guilt free out there participating in saving lives and staying clean doing it. I'm being the vehicle for something bigger. I appreciate my life again, thank you Great Creator.

It is time for sleep. I have a demanding couple of weeks coming up and of course my diversion of having a man to meet for coffee is just that. A diversion from workaholism. I experience all these different ways to run from my feelings; work, men, coffee dates, sugar, shopping, and gambling. The Narcotics Anonymous Basic Text has taught me that "One is too many and a thousand is never enough". I know this intellectually, but emotionally I keep running. I do not want to experience boredom. No regret. No remorse. No grief. No, I do not want to ever feel I am not good enough. Therefore, I stay busy. I avoid, I run, I play. I go to meetings. I help others. I am a perfectionist. I watch a lot of movies. Then it is time for sleep, and I feel. I feel all the feelings; joy, pain, regret, grief, pride, and laughter. I think about online dating, and I feel hope.

26 FOUR DAVID'S – JUNE 2016

This could be it! I'm pumped. I met David. Ooh, ahhh, I like him. Dang, that is certainly a good start. I have not experienced an exciting date in a while.

I am back on Match.com. I find it hard to believe there are three David's with whom I am currently communicating. Then up pop's a message from sixty-two-year-old, David, on POF.com. Weird. Now there are four. Keeping them all straight in name is easy. The rest, not so much.

The first David is HopingSun on Match.com. He is cute, fun, and playful. I have been communicating with him for just over a month. While we had a spark on paper, he did not ask me to coffee. Rather than take the initiative to ask him, I just notice.

His not asking me out speaks loudly. If I were the first to pick up the phone and call, I would at least initiate coffee. This appears to be someone on a dating site who is not actually interested in dating. I am left wondering if he's unavailable. Whatever the reason, he is not moving forward.

The last time I initiated the coffee date, three dates later I was at his house and in his bed only to never hear from him again. He was not interested in a relationship, despite his seeking a long-term relationship on paper. This time I am noticing and even though I would like to say, "hey, what the heck, shall we ever meet?" Instead, I just notice and know it is not going anywhere.

The second David did ask me to call him. I got scared while pursuing him. I am not really attracted, and I know it. At first it was a neutral thing. I communicated with David #two for a couple of weeks only to really find I do not feel the spark. He is military, I am a pacifist. He is about to retire. I am a long way from that place in my life. His pictures online are all twenty plus years old, and I hate that. The current picture is not attractive.

I keep meeting people I am not drawn to with the thought that maybe they are not photogenic or maybe they'll grow on me. The fact is I must stop dating people when there is no spark. I tell myself that in person I will become interested or in time... Or if I can see their personality then I could become interested. It has not worked so far, and it is really awful to be rejected or to reject someone, especially when I've known there hasn't been a spark since the beginning.

I disappear from David #two's life and he will probably talk about my ghosting him to the person that does meet him for coffee. Many online daters talk about their other dating experiences on their first dates with me. I do not feel great about ghosting him, but I am okay with it too. I will keep working out the kinks on how to handle this better in the future. Physical attraction is okay, but an emotional attraction or some kind of spark needs to exist prior to meeting.

David #three is a hoot. For a week we have been

texting daily and I thought it was closer to a month. There are a lot of texts, but no real initiation of a coffee date. Again, I can't stand that. It is not right to go deeper and deeper into thoughts based strictly on imagination. I do not sense he wants to meet; he only likes to text. Strange how so many men want to be online dating just to text. I suppose it does serve its purpose to keep someone from feeling lonely, but I do not want a pen pal.

David #three sent me the first 'real' text telling me about himself in a deeper way, naturally, while I was on a date with David #four. Since David #four began to work out I quit texting with David #three like I'm being loyal or something to David #four now. This is weird since I haven't met anyone, and loyalty is subjective in the dating game.

David #four was charming, and I knew it at once. Cute and thoughtful, a man of faith. Lovely. Maybe a little too serious, but hey, nobody is perfect. I loved our date, shared a lot of great and 'real' stuff. Now I cannot quit thinking about him, and that, my friends, is a spark. Maybe it's obsession but in any case, thank-you, Creator, for placing this man of God in my life. I like this so far.

What I like about David #four is that he is tall (6'5"), he is kind, he is a man of faith, and he is cute. There is something soothing about how he talks, which makes me think he is mindful and gentle. I notice how he compliments me in person and online and I know he likes me, too. This is so exciting!

During our dinner date he said he doubts a relationship is going to work out because he works the graveyard shift and must sleep all the time. I let him know that is not an issue for me because I have a flexible schedule and can do morning dates or evening dates. In fact, my boss is putting the pressure on me to move out of day shift into swing as he wants me available to be the night shift consultant. That only makes sense, and hey, this relationship is not out of the question.

I hear David #four's words of doubt and I reassure him, but I am not sure he is hearing me. Whatever happened in his last eight-month relationship has shaped his thinking that he is stuck, unable to have a relationship. I let that be his belief, but I am determined to continue to reassure him it is not an issue for me.

I find myself thinking, dang what bad timing. This spark is so awesome and yet in three days I am leaving for a week. This is a tough time not to keep the spark alive, but heck, I am looking for a husband who wants to eventually retire together, but how do we keep this crucial spark alive without immediate follow up? I make it a point to text him the next day and we chat by text, and he eventually says he will talk to me when I get back and to keep in touch. Whoop whoop. I hope this spark can stay alive or be revived a week from now.

I know it is important not to lose touch when I travel, so I sent him a John Denver song in a text, "All my bags are packed / I'm ready to go" / and no response. All day. The next day I add, "I'm standing here / outside your door /" and I chit chat about my training going well with a photo of my temporary home, a beautiful skyscraper in Chicago. He texts back, looks like a nosebleed so tall, I'm glad everything went well talk to you when you get back.

That was day two of my incredible trip to different parts of Chicago, IL, Denver and Vail, CO. Okay, so he's not a texter. I get that. It is going to be hard to keep this alive since we only met once, and he does not want to communicate until I get back. Darn.

You can bet I was relieved when he responded that he would call me later after I texted him when I got home. Yes! That night we had a great conversation. It sounds like all he cares about is if I am flexible about his schedule and I reassure him it's all good. I like to go to breakfast, I like to go for walks, I can be spontaneous. In the back of my mind, I wonder if he really does sleep-or try to sleep all day, five days a week. Then I go back to being lighthearted, in the moment, and I am excited he is pumped to give us a try.

He says he has somewhat of a difficult schedule, usually goes to bed at noon or 1:00 pm and starts work at 1:00 am. I assume he is off at 9:30 am and I am thinking, hey, with my upcoming swing shift that could work out. I let him know I am available in the mornings and/or evenings and once again reassure him I can be flexible and that I would like to get to know him. He lets me know his schedule.

The next day he does an unexpected thing. He sent me a message on Match.com. This is strange since the progression of online dating usually does not go in that direction. First, you chat on the site. Then, you decide to meet for coffee. Next, possibly exchange numbers. Then, you only go back to the site to break up, if at all. I am confused now as he sends me this great message about what a special person I am, and he is impressed with the work I do. I replied to him how kind he is and the like. He does not respond after that.

Another day goes by, and he texts me that he is unable to meet with me for a few weeks as his finances are very low. He says we can meet when his bills are lower, but we can talk and share if you like.

Really? That is so disappointing. I am not out to find material for this book I began to write, but I sure do get material I can use. Seriously? You want to be a pen pal? Your ad says you are looking for someone to marry. You are not a very good pen pal frankly.

It appears I am more into him than he is into me. Either this or he has convinced himself that he cannot have a relationship because he only sleeps and works. The other possibility is that the woman of eight-months he was trying to make it work with is still in the picture. Then, maybe he is not over her.

I finish the closure with, I'm not looking for a pen pal. I don't care if we go for a walk, you don't need to spend money on me. I get the distinct impression you are not interested in spending time together which is sad because I like you. Let me know if you change your mind or if I am off base here. Take care, Dave. Karen

He responds, You are a very nice lady, but we are not a good fit. You take care as well and good luck in your search. Dave. This is usually done after the first date on Match.com.

Ouch. I hate rejection. It is either me doing the rejecting or someone else. It is painful. How could he not be interested? Is it possible it is not about me? I would like to be wise enough to know that in my soul, but when this pattern continues for twenty-four years, damn, I must examine the common denominator. Me.

Could I possibly ever be good enough? This insecure part of me that is tapped into at times like this is so uncomfortable to examine. It triggers times in my childhood where I was invisible, neglected, and dominated. Unwanted. Not enough. I was handed my lack of worth from others and believed their assessment.

The trauma at the center of my universe. Here I am traveling across the country by myself, learning more about culture, people, and life than I ever dreamt possible. I am a National Trainer in a scarce field, I run a non-profit for fun, work two jobs, and I hold two licenses that took a decade to earn. Being clean and sober for so long, I have changed. I am present for my life. I am part of something greater that uses me as Its vehicle, and boom. One lousy "not a good fit" text and I'm feeling worth less. Rejected by a stranger in a strange land. Again.

I almost got to the point where I thought I had a boyfriend, again. Oops, too eager. I must wear a sign on my forehead that says, Do Not Pick Me. Then again, I do wonder if God is doing for me what I cannot do for myself. My picker is broken.

Perhaps I should marry my gay, crazy, messed up, drug-using, sex addict, friend; one of my best buddies, Teddy. I love him so much despite his flaws and he loves me back. Thank-you, God, for Teddy. Teddy wants me in his life, he hears me, he sees me, and he loves me. If only he were straight, clean and sober, and free from gambling. He has proposed to me in hopes of giving me good health insurance for the rest of my life. It's tempting.

27 GRATITUDE – SUMMER 2016

I do know I must concentrate on what I am grateful for. I have love, I have known love, I give love, and I am love. Love is all there is.

I am grateful for my Chocolate Lab, Lucky. Also, for my self-employment experience in being able to travel across the United States training Domestic Violence Advocates on how to work with Recovering Survivors. I am ecstatic about my super-duper newly painted cute house. I bought my home as a graduation present to myself. No gratitude outweighs the love and appreciation I have for my awesome son. I am grateful for my two fabulous siblings still living and the two that died. I am grateful for what my parents taught and did for me. I am grateful for water. I'm grateful for my health. I am grateful for all the wonderful and even my not so wonderful old lady clothes I own. I am grateful for my washer and dryer, having enough money, enough food, and a safe neighborhood.

I'm grateful for all the girlfriends, sponsors and

sponsees, and sobriety friends. Especially for all the times I've felt loved by another, both intimate and otherwise. I have had so many close friends, and still do, and I don't take them for granted. Not all my friendships with girlfriends have worked out, but I'm still better for having known the closeness.

I have known love and lust and long for it now. I find it difficult to be content with online dating and being alone when I feel I still have much to give and share.

I keep myself busy with real friends and acquaintances. I get through the mundane by getting all caffeinated up, by singing and laughing with my people, and by going out to play regularly. Probably in the future caffeine will be seen as a drug by recovering people, but for now it is an acceptable form of a high. Drinking a few Chai Latte's or an occasional Red Bull makes me let go of my inhibitions, cut loose, and dance. When I get real though, I do know I am tuning out, not tuning in or being present. I run from the pain of being alone and disconnected. I pretend all those high-fives are the real deal.

Keith is a leader at my church and in my recovery circle. I read a book he wrote about his drug using days and felt a lot of different emotions. I hated him for the self-admitted jerk that he was and for how he thought. Yet it is familiar, and I'm drawn to it. The selfish, self-centered egotistical excuse for a man, only out for himself, and unable to see how he affects others. It bothers me to the extreme. He's such a con artist which I hate because he is just like my father. This is familiar. I do wonder if I have a finger pointed out if the remaining three fingers are pointed at me for a reason.

Single and Sober: Who Found My Slipper?

Then I start to generalize…all men are self-centered egomaniacs like Keith and my dad, which I don't truly believe. Still, I'm barely ready to look at myself as selfish, self-centered, and egotistical. Keith's journey has been so much like mine. I had no clue how I came across to others, unaware my selfish motives were harmful.

I begin to see what Keith and I have in common. Especially from the spiritual realm. From simple recovery-based prayers, "God please keep me clean" to experiencing meta-physical dimensions like I've found in women's sweat lodges and in meditation. I begin to work on letting go of the rocks, the character defects like judgment, anger, fear, and selfishness. I am learning to serve others.

Keith and I, we get excited to be still and find peace. Then we share the job that comes when we get to spread peace throughout the universe. I hate him and I love him. It is my dark side and my light that we share in finding we are in Unity and all there is-is Love. That light that shines within us is the Sunlight of the Spirit.

I need not search for something I already have. I want to strengthen my connection. Love deeper, spend time and energy in being still, and be a vehicle for God's love. I often wonder if this is my higher power's plan as I must admit my way is not working. I need to continue to practice letting go and letting God. What I'm looking for is not out there. As Cat Stevens would sing, "The answer lies within / So why not take a look now? / Get out, get out, get out / the Good Book now / Then I found myself one day / When I wasn't even trying".

That is it. I must quit trying. Love isn't out there. I know that. I cannot expect anyone to fill my cup and I do know this. I want to get my love from the Source. I eventually learned from the teachings in the book Alcoholic Anonymous to pray. God, please help me drop the rocks, my character defects, and be available to connect with the Sunlight of The Spirit. I want to get rid of the blockage that stands in the way of myself and God. Let go of the resentments, the fear, the selfishness, and the ego. I want to be a vehicle of love. Namaste'.

28 MUSIKY – AUGUST 2016

A couple months have lapsed, and I've been uninterested in communicating online. I do not want to look for more of the same disappointment from the dating scene. However, I noticed a note-to-self to close my Match.com account before the 3 months expires and they charge me again. A few days prior to leaving I sent a couple emails just because the account was ending, and I had a nice response from Musiky. Since I love music and so does he, and we are from the same era, I think, hey, perhaps I've met my match. There is not a whole lot I like better than sitting around playing songs from the 70's and connecting through music.

We had a live chat, and it went really well. We are connecting in a way I've been looking for. Gosh, just when I was about to give up, too. He doesn't want to end the chat and neither do I, so we keep saying good-bye and then he says, and one more thing, and I giggle and stay up way past my bedtime and it's worth it. One more thing becomes several, then I have one more thing. God works in mysterious ways, for sure. We exchange phone numbers and I'm getting excited, which is hard to do since I'm cynical at best and bored with this type of dating at worst.

The very next day he calls me and I'm working but I take the call and decide a break is in order. The 15 minutes whips by and I'm not liking what I am hearing. When I asked about his guitar and particular interest in genres, he gave me a ten-minute answer that had little to do with guitar, music, or taste. He didn't really play guitar. He had a collector guitar he is proud of and once changed the strings. This time when I said I was working he said, one more thing, and went on for ten more minutes and there was no respect for the fact that I was working. I said, I have to go now several times in the last ten minutes of the call. I am so off base in picking seriously mentally ill men.

My idea of wanting to click with someone makes me blind to reality. This is Karen, not God, creating a fantasy and turning another boy with concerning issues into my Prince Charming. I hated to let him down, but I wasn't about to continue this any further. I Googled how to end an online dating relationship and got some great and simple ideas. I went back to Match.com and told him straight up. I think you're a nice guy but not for me. He left me a ten-minute voicemail agreeing and he decided since I'd played music on stage in the past and that he didn't, that was my deal breaker. Okay, we all need a story that makes sense to us. He wasn't devastated and I did my duty of not leaving him hanging. I closed my Match.com account and am totally fine with that decision.

In fact, I'm moving more into my Buddhist Recovery ways and practices. I am enjoying being in my own skin more, being less busy, sending light and love to others, and simply being loving and kind to myself. I do not need a companion to make me happy. Seriously, for the first time in my life I am alone and truly enjoying it. Sure, I get bored, go to a meeting, and come home to the animals. Not in a lonely pathetic way, though. More by choice.

Companions have irritated me in recent years more than filling my lonely cup. Cat sitting my son's exotic F4 Savannah kitten has been exciting. Watching Leo, or Leonardo DaVinci, the sleek and precious, rare, and wild kitty, play with my chocolate lab, Lucky, is such a joy. I could sit and watch them all day. In fact, I have for the past two days. I'm like a crazed Grandma with the videos, pictures, and Facebook posts.

I found myself annoyed having to leave the animals to follow up with life's obligations. Watching this three-pound leopard descendant chase the equivalent size tail of my fifty-pound lab is more desirable. Leo leaps like a rabbit and pounces like his ancestors, the leopards. He's so little his attacks are entertaining and cute instead of scary and deadly. Leo's markings are that of extraordinary rosettes and his behavior unique. He is more like a dog than a cat in many ways. Leo even walks on a leash! Loyal, friendly, cuddly, and so playful. I left for work but thought about the pets all night long as I barely listened to people talk about suicide on the crisis line. Except when they were serious, of course.

29 MARIO, PHIL, AND JAMES - FALL 2016

Then, I received a notice by email. Four-hours of FREE dating app Chemistry.com. I am working, but figure what the heck. If I get a minute, I'll give out my email address and see if any sparks flow. I expect nothing and know I can block unwanted predators if needed. I need a distraction from working the night shift as a supervisor now at the Crisis Line. I posted a cute little profile that takes three minutes. I get a list of the people I have chemistry with before I even select preferences or go searching. It appears as if Match.com and Chemistry.com are the same company. They've reposted my picture and my profile, and included the mistake I made when I listed my income bracket. I took that off at once as I was unsure what I was thinking. I do not want to be vulnerable to guys seeking my money. No cat phishing allowed in my universe.

Not that I'm floating in cash working in Human

Services. My tax bracket hasn't changed a lot since the seventh grade. I would love to pair up with another professional. However, a loser looking for a woman to support him is the more likely vulnerability with online dating. It doesn't feel right to be so exposed. Glad I could remove the income listing right off the bat.

Again, my heart was pumping as I got three immediate emails, which I didn't expect. Usually, I get a wink. Period. I'm getting super nice, detailed emails from people wanting to know more about me. They read my profiles, too, as they were responding to things that caught their attention like my eyes and my positive outlook. Sometimes you get these generic emails that are probably sent to many women. These messages seem different. All three men are cute as can be and seem to be professional. Woo-hoo, yahoo, finally! Now that the site is free, I am seeing some potential candidates. I'm not out of the dating scene, I just hadn't had many potential hopefuls and now I have three. It is all or nothing I swear.

I print out all that I can about these men and our correspondence since my ability to rescope out their profiles ends in a couple hours. I send them my email address as I am printing their information. I see the website has turned both mine and their email addresses into *****.com to encourage joining rather than communicating directly. I don't expect the correspondence to continue. After this free four-hour session, much to my surprise all three guys sent me an email so we could continue communicating. Oh my gosh, this is fun and exciting!

It's even more thrilling in between speaking to depressed callers and/or dispatching designated county mental health responders to crises in progress. I am allowed to be distracted online during my work time. This job is impossible to do without diversion from the intensity of being part of the first responder team.

I am disappointed that my normal filter of a fifty-mile radius was not in place during this free evening on Chemistry.com. Looking closer, the cutie patootie named Gene is listed as from Vancouver, BC, about four hours north. He tells me he goes by the name of Mario. He quotes Gandhi and speaks of mindfulness and healthy communities. Oh yes, a director in personality traits, he enjoys dance, and he's ready to embrace possibilities. He is an engineer who enjoys running, yoga, hiking, holistic health, and spiritual practices, including meditation. Ooh la la.

This is exactly the profile I am drawn to. I can hear his British Canadian accent and I'm drowning in fantasy before we even converse. I do know not to trust all people from the internet or other countries as it can involve cat phishing. I am not interested in becoming a victim of that. Let's take this slow and see if he's for real. I want to know why he calls himself Mario and lists his name as Gene.

The next is NewDayPhil. An Irishman who lives in the same small town as I, Marysville, WA. Oh yes, a gorgeous hunk with a brain. Here is Phil's message. I include the messages verbatim.

I never guessed I'd try online dating, but here I am… I am intrigued by your profile and our common interests. You have gorgeous eyes and your smile made my day. Please drop me a line cause I'm not too comfortable talking about my personal life through the website. Hope you'll give me a change to get to know you better… You're an "Explorer" and I'm a "Negotiator" and based on Dr. Fisher's research we have charm to spare and will naturally get along. You're spontaneous and creative, I'm flexible and imaginative. We are both in store for some great adventures and hearty laughs together.

I remember only trying Chemistry.com once when it was new. I was seeking a male and they matched me with a female twenty years my junior. I thought it was a hoax but was left wondering if maybe I'm in denial and I'm homophobic. This could be, I really love women. Only I haven't found the kind of spark my Prince Charming, real or imagined, seems to evoke from my body toward females. It's more about admiration and I think I want to be **like** certain women, more than I want to be **with** them. I believe being a lesbian or being straight lies more on a continuum than only on far extremes. I lean more toward liking males, but to me love isn't about gender as much as it is about passion, attraction, and interests.

Now I realize Phil is a tall, handsome, 6' 2", and he cooks. That sparks me. He reads and is athletic/toned. Yeah, I'm thinking I would love to explore negotiating with Phil. Plus, he's fifty-seven and seeks a woman forty-five to sixty-six. Some of these old guys are seeking girls, wanting twenty-to-thirty-year-olds. It's a sick society that encourages old men to pair up with girls. They are not the men for me. Not only am I not a child, but I also don't care for men who buy into that sick thinking. Phil says he's looking for a woman, even an older woman, and more likely my type. I just hope he's not looking for a mother.

Then there is James, also from out of the area. He's a hottie from Hillsboro, Oregon, near where my son's dad lives, nearly four hours south of Marysville. James knows exactly what to say. He loves my smile and loses his breath looking deep into my eyes. It would be his pleasure to start a conversation with a beautiful lady like me. My eyes have always been my best feature. He wants to know more. Well, I do too. Who are you James and why did it take us so long to find one another? Tell me more.

In just a few hours of Chemistry.com there are now a few prospects as future partners. There is Gene, who goes by Mario, from Vancouver, BC. I love that accent! There is Phil from the greater Seattle area, the most realistic because he lives in my small town, Marysville, Washington. Then there is James from Hillsborough, Oregon, who lives near my ex. I started emailing each of them and look forward to seeing how it goes.

Gene, fifty-five, from Vancouver, BC, aka Mario. After an exchange of email addresses, I continue the dialogue while confirming my email address:

"Hi Mario, Yes, you did get my email correct! That's great. Yes, tell me more about yourself. What do you do for fun? What's your favorite animal? What are you doing today? Have a great day. Karen" This is Mario's response:

Hello Karen...

Hope your day is going fine and you're not working yourself too hard? Thank you so much for the reply.i really appreciate,thout I'd tell you more about myself and you do the same and we can take it from there? Well here go,its not easy talking about one's self but I will try.

I'm a Construction/Civil Engineer, I'm into building and constructions, I handle my job in contracts because I am self employed.... My parents were full Italians,though from different states..They are both of blessed memories now..I was born in the suburb of VeRoberta in Italy but I don't speak Italian but understand a little. I have an ascent cause I left when I was very young after the death of my father,myself and my mom actually relocated to England after he died..Actually granduated from the university of Sheffield.

I'm a single dad blessed with a lovely girl.,I got married 18 years ago and it lasted for just 10 years, My divorce was quite difficult because never saw it coming. My daughter is 17 years, she schools in Manchester, England because I have a home there also, she is in her first year of medical college and she wants to be a dentist, nothing makes me happier....The last time I heard about my ex-wife was that she was involved in a car accident with her lover and she was in critical condition because they were both on drugs and she was an alcoholic, she hasn't seen our daughter for 3 years,I wonder how some women can be so heartless enough to abandon their own child, well my daughter is fine now,she is growing into a beautiful woman and she completes me.

I am artistic and with a good sense of humor,quick witted, friendly , energetic and I do my best to keep my emotions in balance. I have not felt the love of woman for long nowmand I really miss it,to be sincere ,I'm quite scared, but just want to be bold. As the saying goes, no risk, no reward. I'm taking the risk of meeting someone, trusting and i know that there is someone out there for me..I love to cook and pasta is what I cook more,do you like pasta?

Well, I will stop here for now and waiting for your reply cause i would really appreciate getting to know you more also,please tell me about yourself?

Have a lovely day.
Hope to hear from you soon.
Mario

At first glance this is sweet. This guy could be exotic and loving; someone who needs a good woman to love. All the finest traits; humble, hardworking, motivated, loyal, an Italian Stallion. Italian with an English accent, okay!!! I begin to drool. A stable man, proud of his daughter, the Dentist, who he raised alone. Scared, but willing to risk loving again, despite an ex-who abandoned him and his daughter.

But I have seen too many of these types of messages. I do not for a minute believe this man. His English is broken, and he tells me right off he has a home overseas. We are not talking four hours north of me like he advertised. I highly doubt he is living in Vancouver, Canada. This is someone cat phishing, and I would lay money on it, even though I'm trying not to gamble these days. The biggest flag to me is that he hasn't answered any of my questions. This is a pat email. Patented. Most likely this has been sent to many American women to see who's vulnerable enough to take the cat phishy fish bait which will ultimately result in sending money. Who is hungry enough? No. My Italian Stallion Gene or Mario, whoever you are. You smell.

Secretly, I doubt my decision and wonder if I am too hypersensitive and ruling out every possible mate because I enjoy being alone. It is a fact that all humans have flaws and I seem to spot them, and the potential of a sham is enough for me to shoo them away. Hmm. I'll find a therapist and may discuss this someday. But right now, I have two other pursuers.

Single and Sober: Who Found My Slipper?

Phil, 57, Marysville, WA is interesting as he is new to online dating, he's cute, and he's local. I like the innocence of his profile and his personal note to me. I like that he's Irish, I'm most familiar with my own culture. I relate to the dry humor and the dry drunk. Ha-ha. I'd prefer it if they work a recovery program though. I should get out of my comfort zone more. The comfort of an Irishman is like wearing my favorite old sneakers.

Comfy, but sometimes they need to be tossed aside for a fresh new pair. I do like dating men different from my own white race and European ancestry, too. It has helped me see my own privilege, learn about my prejudices, and notice the color of one's skin or how they celebrate holidays is to be honored. Difference is not to be feared. I embrace these opportunities. I also notice the way we are treated differently by people of my own race. Embarrassing. Infuriating. Appalling.

I go through the typical Yes, you have the right email! How are you? process and here is Phil's response: *Good morning Karen,*

Much thanks to you for the answer and I trust you had a lovely night. You look charming and conventional. I need you to know that I am Originally from Dublin, Ireland. I moved to Canada seven years prior, for more Job open doors and to Stay Permanently I have lived in New York for 6 years before moving to Washington. My field of work is designing, into a building and work developments. I am independently employed and I handle my business in contracts. I have a 28 year old girl name Meryl. She lives in Dublin, soon to get Married. She is the highlight of my life. I have 'not been in any relationship since I lost my wife. I would prefer only not to hurry into any relationship that won't keep going long, I need a relationship that can prompt something awesome, I am prepared to move closed to the right lady. I have had a progression of employments in the past and I believe it's chance to assemble a relationship too. I am a moderately cordial individual that can be the focal point of a discussion or sit on the sideline and feel fine in either part. Solid active ladies are a turn on. I adore Happy ladies who recognize what is going ahead on the planet. Affection to go out to supper and the motion pictures. Very little into clubs, yet cherish a nearby bar and unrecorded music. Satire clubs are a decent redirection, affection to watch great motion pictures at home on a snuggled up night. Games are an absolute necessity, yet I won't lounge around throughout the day observing any of them. I figure I can't sit still sufficiently long. Love the opposition of some specific games. Top picks incorporate soccer.

I am a man who will never undermine my accomplice on the grounds that I trust that God made one man for one lady thus I ought to be similar to that. Kindly wouldn't fret my long story.
God favor
Phil

Now my heart is beating fast. Phil is so cute and lives in my small town. I love the fact that he's from Dublin! I prefer someone who's new to online dating. I'm leery that Phil is really attracted when the best he could call me is "conventional", not sure if that's a compliment. I am unsure if some of his word choices are due to his being raised in Dublin or if it's an elite thing. I never put down my income before and now I'm getting some interesting wealthy men turning their attention my way.

Single and Sober: Who Found My Slipper?

I'm not sure if the disconnect is cultural due to socio economic class or growing up on different continents. Heck I can talk trailer trash. Just don't put me in a Golf Course Country Club setting and expect me not to curse. I decide to learn more about Phil with the following email: "Hi Phil,

Thank you for your great email! I can almost hear it with your Canadian/New York/Irish accent, lol. My ancestry is from Ireland. I visited there in the eighties and loved it. I grew up in Michigan, lived a decade in Florida then came out to the Northwest in the late eighties and settled down. I have a twenty-five-year-old son whom I adore that lives near me. I look forward to becoming a grandmother one day but for now I'm his car sitter:) I went to college in my thirties to figure out how to afford to raise my son on my own when my relationship with his dad ended. I've been climbing in the Human Services/Social Work ladder since and landed comfortably in a management position near my home, finally. The traffic and commute to Seattle is grueling! I also have my own business and travel nationally on occasion to train other human service professionals. I am spiritually grounded in God, I am happy, and I am an extrovert who also enjoys observing. Enough about me. Tell me more about your designing building work. What are you most proud of? When did you lose your wife (sorry to hear that). I look forward to hearing from you.

Fondly,
Karen"

Darn typo's I'm not car sitting, I'm cat sitting. Urgh. Well, I've done my fair share of car sitting for my son who's left his broken-down cars in my driveway. I guess that's accurate. It can't be odder than calling me conventional. Maybe I am the polyester kind. My work wardrobe is taking over my life and I go to NA meetings wearing that kind of crap. Maybe I am seen as conventional. Oh my. I have changed in my twenty-four years of recovery. I was a blue jean baby queen and now I'm a conventional dresser. Do I ever get to be cool? Leather & lace kind of cool?

Where's Teddy and the glove we found downtown Chicago? At first, we thought it was black lace underwear. When we figured out it was a glove, I wore it all day and felt so cool strutting down Michigan Avenue with my high tops, rolled up jeans, and one black lace glove. Dancing down the Magnificent Mile with my proud gay friend, laughing, and being silly. Doing the Queen's wave with my newly found black lace fingerless glove was a memory forever embedded into my brain.

Let's see if Phil writes back. He may like the conventional type. Just don't call me Republican. I have my deal breakers. I have been known to love some Republican's, but they would probably not be a good match for me as a partner at this point in my life.

Ahh, I have male. I mean mail. Oh goodness, I didn't respond in four hours, and I have four emails awaiting. This was a great idea to get the free Chemistry.com evening. Let me sneak a peek from Phil's response:

Good evening Karen,

Much obliged to you for giving me a chance to have your time and consideration. I feel retired, delighted in expecting your mail, exceptionally fascinating. I am having a really decent evening with myself, you should? I just thought I'd impart my experience to you to empower you know me more. I was brought forth in Dublin, Ireland. Feb 26th, 1959, I originated from a white collar class foundation. My mom is from Turkey while my father is from Dublin, Ireland. I hold double citizenship(Irish and Turkish). My dad has worked an assortment of employments, yet he winds up in Mechanical building Before he passed on at age 83 that was three years back.

A companion of mine brings me into a chemistry.com yet I never discovered enthusiasm for it. I accept there will be a ton of Games in it, just to give an attempt on it only for once. I have an exceptionally open heart and as a free-minded individual, I need to open my heart for somebody that can deal with it with consideration from her heart, cos I'm apprehensive about the disaster I don't care for pondering my past any longer. I was hitched to my late wife for more than 26 years, she bites the dust 10 years prior thought Brain turmoil, my mother was filling in as a maternity care for the administration doctor's facility, she was the lady, despite the fact that She dead Last year. I was near my guardians, I was there just tyke, they generally attempt to give all that I need to me. I was raised up as a Christian. My Dad was working in Istanbul that is the way he implied my mother. I conceived in Turkey till I was 16 years of age, then I moved to Dublin with my Family to proceed with my college training, I cleared out Dublin 7 years back to US for a Job...I am not a material person. Someday I would like to help individuals make healthier, all the more adoring choices with their lives.. I adore everything about my development work, I am into the development of oil pipelines, clinics, development of streets and building of structures for organizations. I scarcely get irate on the grounds that I do trust that vitality and time ought to be into something great.

For now and a debt of gratitude is in order for the perusing trust that you don't discover anything hostile in what I have composed, if there is whatever else you might want to know, kindly don't keep down to pose any Question and I might want to know more about you.

Anticipating you're sweet reaction
Phil

I received three messages from Phil, with all the same body. Weird. I also received one from James in OR that I'm anxious to read, too.

I'm confused as I converse with both Phil and Mario simultaneously who is the building designer and who works independently and if that means they are on contracts or just unemployed. I can see that word choices, like feeling retired and delighted in the same sentence, are unusual. I'm seeing the explanation that Phil was raised in Turkey. My Irishman is starting to show his blarney side. I'm on to him. I reread the other emails and see that Phil and Mario could be the same guy.

They both design buildings, work independently, and have a daughter who is going to need him soon who just happens to be in a far-away land. English is not their first language, which is not a turn off for me. However, pretending to be someone you are not to steal someone's heart and soon enough their money, well that turns me off. The whole reason I'm so drawn to Phil is because he's Irish and lives in Marysville. Hmm. Turns out he's not really Irish, he's Turkish who is prepared to move close to the right lady. Really? How much closer to Marysville

Single and Sober: Who Found My Slipper?

would you move, Phishy Phil? Perhaps you could kiss the Blarney Stone on your way. You are not a material guy. I'm guessing that is true. You are seeking someone else's materials and that doesn't make you a good builder. Maybe a good designer, though. Oh darn, I was so looking forward to some good old fashion Irish stories.

James, fifty-eight, Hillsboro, OR. A good Irish name. The name of my father and my brother. My father the bi-polar man with a borderline personality, good ole' Irish storyteller and my brother the cocaine addicted middle child who wore the weight of the emotional turmoil of our family. Yeah, I like Jim's. My uncles, my cousins, my neighbors, my ex's. I know about Jim's, and they are not phishing in Africa or Turkey.

Not that all cat phishers are from Nigeria, but my friend Dalia's cat phisher was, and he totally got her good. Bad. Whatever. He stole her heart and wanted her money. A private detective found his computer address in NY was actually just pit stopping in NY and originating from Nigeria.

Again, I am an explorer and Jim is a director. We are unconventional, energetic, and daring. Ah, he must be a bad boy. We have many shared interests and will have a deep intellectual focus according to Dr. Fisher. Another Irish person who is in the know that I certainly can understand.

Jim sent me the sweetest message, "A note from James":

I find it very interested reading your profile. You have a lovely smile on your face, that really attracted me the most and I nearly lost my breath looking deep into your eyes. I like your hair style a lot and I am just sitting here *wondering what a beautiful angel like you is doing on here. Anyway we ar3e looking and it will be my pleasure to start a conversation with a beautiful lady like you. I don't know much about you. I will be glad to get to know each other better. I'm not very active on this site but then you can contact me on *****. I'm very big on texting, Lol. Or kindly write me*****yahoo.com. I appreciate and admire your intensity hope to hear from you soon, James*

I am attracted and send him the following response:
Hi James,

What a very sweet message you sent! Thank you.

I usually don't communicate with people from outside my area, however, your note is so personal and kind I couldn't resist. My son's father lives in Aloha, so I'm familiar with your area, but we are quite a distance apart.

I would be interested in emailing also, for starters, but this site blocked your email address. Try me at karenf***dot com.
Karen from Marysville, WA (Close to Everett).

Miraculously he finds me even though the site is blocking my address. I just don't get this technology today.

Thanks for your nice compliment and interest.Well, I was born and raised by strong parents in Trinidad and Tobago, West Indies, came to Cleveland, OH at age 34, been here since, just move Hillsboro, OR. I am a hot spicy Caribbean man with the North American flavor and a blend of many other flavors - You might be glad you did. Try to think happy thoughts you will be surprise how well it works. I am flexible and willing to try anything at least once.

Single and Sober: Who Found My Slipper?

I'm a widower father of a 17 years old son. He is Stann by name.. My late wife died through a congestive heart disease. It was a great lost because she was a wonderful mother and wife both to me and Stann respectively. I have raised my son so far on my own and have not dated much since the lost of my wife. I have focused on trying to raise my son and keep him on a straight path in life. He is the source of my happiness and the love of my life. He has more knowledge in Economics, Science and Mathematics.

I am into telecommunications. I take contracts involving the mounting and setting up of telecommunication systems, challenging at times but i thrive on challenges.. I own my home and private office. I lost my mom when she was under taking a back surgery in 1999. My dad died of Cancer in 1987. As an only child, they taught me how to be soo much about caring for people and accepting them as who they are .. respect, honor,dignity, honesty,compassion,and love.. were some of the strongest features that were instilled in me.I like to take things at their natural rhythm when it comes to relationships.

I like a balanced life with both the reaching big and the down to earth simple things and way of being. I love deep, intelligent conversation (a great sense of humor is a must), dinners, happy hours and foot massages...low key nights watching TV or more active nights out Dancing. Well, I truly want to get the opportunity to get to know you, all of you. Head, Heart, Spirit, and Soul. I look forward to hear from you soon.
I Care,
James

PS. What I do for fun..I Love the movies, walking,long discussions on whatever takes our fancy, quiet ambiance, most musical styling, going to the gym, reading, hanging out low-key or fancy, writing,traveling sometimes head to an exotic beach to listen to the waves, my favorite animal is Dog. what am up too, still in my office taking care of a few pages of paperwork.

Well, James from Aloha, Trinidad, wherever, you at least added a PS to answer my questions. I bet you are taking care of a few pages of paperwork. Hacking, phishing, moving from Vancouver to NY to England to Turkey to Trinidad and Tabago of the West Indies. How do you keep it all straight? I am now convinced this online dating is not the way to meet my soulmate, but it has been entertaining. I am certain the free four-hour Chemistry.com was hacked, also.

At this moment I am going to stop my son's curious exotic cat from disturbing my paperwork, hop in the shower, and go to my Buddhist Recovery meeting. I will use the Buddha's teaching to overcome my addiction to the Cinderella fantasy and become present in my life. I am happy. I am well. I am love.

I am going to be loving and kind to myself and stop this online dating nonsense once and for all. I will spend my days noticing all the love in my heart and sitting in meditation to cast my love onto others.

I am on day five out of my fourteen-day goal: to send love toward the four people that I still hold resentments about. Each day tears have welded up in my eyes as I open my heart to love those who have made me angry. I send light and request my defect of being selfish and self-seeking, dishonest and fearful be removed. Then

Single and Sober: Who Found My Slipper?

I pray and practice Metta. I love others and include those people that have done me wrong. I send love to myself, to them, and I do it with intention. How else can there be peace on Earth if it doesn't start with me?

Thank-you God, Buddha, NA, AA, OA, GA, ESR, BR, Nic-Anon, women's sweat lodges on Tulalip Reservation, churches, sponsors, sponsees, meditation teachers all over the world, and all my loving friends and family that give me the strength and wisdom to walk in light and love instead of hate and fear. I am love. I found what I've been looking for! My skin is fitting and comfy.

30 A MOMENT OF CLARITY – AUGUST 2016

It's the eighth month and all the recovery meetings I've been to had something to do with the eighth Step. Write a list and gather a plan to right the wrongs you've done to others. I paraphrase. I do know the anger, the resentments, they all start and end with me. That is sometimes hard to recognize. When I hold onto hate it's like drinking poison and expecting the other person to die. Plus, it blocks me from the sunlight of the spirit and interrupts world peace.

I'd like to think since I am decades into being clean & sober that I'd be over this blockage and be flying in the sunlight of the spirit. By now I should be living in God's will, not my own, just out of habit from practicing good living for so many years. I do know that my serenity is a direct relation to the daily maintenance with my spiritual connection.

My Buddhist Recovery program is asking me to get

real. If my addictions are still active, any of them, then I need to admit I am not Stepping on the path of recovery. I still overeat, I crave sugar, and relapse weekly with loving pastries or whatever I can get my hands on. I am only months clean from gambling, sixteen years off tobacco, and twenty-four years substance free.

But who am I kidding? I may not be doing meth or alcohol, weed or cocaine, but I crave sugar and feed the beast. I am still drawn to dopamine. It's the adrenaline I feel going on dates that offer a potential future with a partner that I'm attracted to, also. Another kind of dope.

Am I really substance free? Am I happy, joyous and free? Some of the time I am. Then I forget. I head to the Casino for some fun seeking external things like sugar, caffeine, or gambling to fill up my internal void. As if dating or other adrenalin seeking methods could fill me up like only my higher power can do. The bells and whistles at the Casino make me forget I'm not connected to the Sunlight of the Spirit. Then I lose money, gain weight, feel like a prisoner to my addictions, and leave desperate and more alone and rejected than when I arrived. I've come to see my brain as that of a whack-a-mole game. I hammer on one addiction and out pops another. It's an endless game of chase without the chance of ever winning because one is too many and a thousand never enough.

I do have resentments, yes. Toward four of my family members. I will start there. I'm on day ten of doing a sort of Buddhist Metta or a mini fourth through eighth Step renewal regarding myself and these four people. The results so far have been moving and enlightening. I have been able to start to see and feel how I have affected them, not just the other way around. It's not just lip service praying for them to be well with the underlying thought, but I'm right. I have come to see that I negatively affected them, and this is due to my character defects of being self-centered, self-seeking, and dishonest.

When I lie to myself about the truth, I'm being dishonest. Each of my actions are based on fear that I will lose my family, exactly where being right and not sorry or apologetic has led. I can only learn from noticing that when I acted alone, calling CPS on my ex-sister-in-law that beats her children, I took the other family members all out of the unity equation. Damn. Good to know and painful to notice my desire to do the right and courageous thing to protect my young nephew. I steam rolled my family that were closest to the situation. Where else do I steam roll people? Have I done this before without noticing and without consideration of how I affect them in my quest to be right?

This morning a new thought came to me, too. I have my list. My list of girlfriends that have become estranged who I believe I had to cut out of my life. Each one involves a story where I am right, they are bad people, they did bad things to me, and whom I will never trust again. Done, over and out. There are a few women that are never going to get my time of day again. It leaves me feeling pain, lonely, angry, hungry. Hmm. It started just prior to my getting clean and sober.

We were the Karen & Kathy club. My partner in crime, my closest friend at the time. She turned me on to crank, also known as speed. She stayed up with me four days at a time regularly, bartending with me at The Stagecoach Saloon outside Portland, Oregon. We were inseparable. My very best friend since Kristy from Florida.

Then she met Dick, the violent jerk face mean guy. She left her sweet alcoholic partner and moved in with Dick. The father of many, dad of none, or so it seemed. She asked me to be her best lady. I refused to be her maid of honor let alone sign for her forever after with the jerk. I boycotted the wedding.

She and my son's dad tried so hard to convince me I was crazy when I got clean. They truly believed that I didn't have a problem. They were both worse off in their addiction and my getting clean made them face that fact. It is not normal to not eat or sleep, to neglect my baby, and to spend half of my life in a blackout. Only by hanging out with people whose life is similar did I think I didn't have a problem. I resented Kathy for not supporting my recovery journey, when I quit drinking and using, despite knowing denial runs deep and she couldn't see the light at that time. Not that I was any better.

I started my recovery by doing a ninth Step with Kathy prior to working the first eight Steps or having a sponsor. "I am so sorry, but if you hadn't hooked up with that guy, I wouldn't have …" Not realizing that I was blaming her for my behavior, I made things worse between us and boom, over. Never to be friends again. Painful. Lonely. Hungry for my friend I can't hang out with anymore if I want to stay clean and sober. I learned never to do a ninth Step without first doing Steps one to eight with a sponsor.

Through Facebook I later learned they spent their lives together and he was there for her and their children. Who am I to judge? I eat my words. I do the Steps in order for a reason.

Another friend & I were very close, like sisters, for

many decades. Roommates at eighteen, vacation buddies for years, she took me in when I was in need. We really loved one another. I helped her get off cocaine, later she helped me get off meth. I always knew she was mean, selfish, and a bully, but I loved her anyway.

At fifteen years clean and sober, I stayed with her for the weekend to help her put on her son's wedding reception. I was disappointed that she turned her guest bedroom, that she always called Karen's room into a pot growing room. She started changing her language to be a medicinal marijuana supplier, a pharmaceutical vendor. That change of language from a dope grower and dealer to medicine supplier made me angry. The early days of medical marijuana were so odd. I was resistant to legitimizing the substance that kept me from growing up or participating in being present in my life for decades. It was my real drug of choice.

We had fifteen years of practice dancing around spending weekends together when she smoked and I didn't, and it was hard for me. Occasionally, I would walk into a scene where she was smoking pot with friends, and she'd get high, forget, and pass me the joint. That weekend she was so proud of her crop she grabbed a handful of buds, stuck them in my nose, and said, smell this! I was triggered and started craving even though her disrespect for my recovery was at the hub. The allergy of my body kicked in and I wanted to both kick her butt and smoke her weed, but I was a sober pacifist too stubborn and angry to give her or myself that satisfaction.

On the way back to Seattle from Portland I was full of 'dis-ease'. I had been triggered when smelling the buds. I wanted a drink so bad it was killing me. I found a meeting in Centralia, WA that I equate with saving my life. To be so mad at her for not respecting my recovery made me want to drink and it made no sense.

I was in pain, grieving, and knowing our friendship was over. I felt lonely and angry. It was over between us. I just can't risk my recovery. She was disrespectful and put my life and sobriety in jeopardy. I'm right. Over. Done. Never again. A twenty-seven-year friendship is over. When I think back, I know why in recovery they say get rid of the old people, playgrounds, and playthings. The only thing you must change in recovery is everything.

In the past, I would not have equated smoking marijuana with being life threatening. Today, I know it's only the tip of the iceberg. The quality of my life would change, and I would be left with the F-its. My identity would be lost. Anything and everything would be okay to do next. I know all this is not about the substance. It's about my broken brain and I can't afford to get the F-its. If I were to smoke weed or drink a beer, I know myself well enough to know the F-its would take over and life as I know it would be over. A spiritual death would kick off the addict/alcoholic within and I would lose my job, my self-esteem, my health, and my friends. No, I can't afford to pick up. Anything.

I can see how selfish I was when I used alcohol and other drugs. I couldn't take other's feelings into account, getting and finding ways and means to stay high became my focus.

Today, I am truly grateful I can notice others. I just wish my recovery was surrounded with more healthy people. It took fifteen years of being clean and sober to let go of this friend that I knew was a danger to my recovery from the start. Even though I love her, I had to let her go if I wanted to stay clean. I still love her, only now it's from a distance and she probably thinks I hate her. I'm still learning how to right the wrongs without putting my recovery in danger. Instead, I stay away. I miss her but I stay healthy.

31 STAN – SEPTEMBER 2016

Stan was one that had potential to notice I seek a proposal on a black stallion, or a white stallion, I am not that picky. Turns out he proposed to his wife in the music filled, sexy town of Port Townsend, WA, overlooking the Pacific Ocean. Oh my, I knew I picked my Prince Charming when my heart fluttered for that gorgeous man. I know he liked me too; he saw what I saw, he felt what I felt. I just wish he hadn't died on me. Well, not *on* me. LOL. We never got that close, darn. Glad he let go of me prior to getting so ill. I could not have grieved him just after my oldest sister and brother died. I would have ended up in the psych ward, for certain. I have felt divinely guided since entering recovery as if my ancestors are making sure I don't get too overwhelmed at any one time.

In fact, that's where Stan ended up just after he let me go. He was suicidal over losing his ability to work, losing his healthy athletic body, losing his ability to take on a serious relationship. He ended up at Fairfax Psychiatric Hospital. Bi-polar. One day we are dating, and the chemistry is clicking, and things are progressing.

Maybe I'm mistaking his mania for passion, just maybe. Our dogs hang out. We walk, we talk, we share. He takes me on a double date with his best friend. He joins my home group. There is nothing sexier than joining my home group, okay. He wants into my world. Ooh, baby ooh, say ooh.

Then, he is literally certifiably crazy. He's manic and I'm his best friend. He's depressed and he doesn't seem to know who I am. It was whiplash love, so confusing. I'm on fire for him and would have followed him to the looney bin or shortly thereafter, the hospital medical ward if he'd let me know prior to his discharge.

I did go visit him once at the hospital when he was admitted for organ failure. That was a big deal as I'd vowed to only visit people in the hospital if they were close family. I brought him his favorite sports magazines and felt like a schoolgirl with the biggest crush ever. I did not know he'd be dead a short time later.

I was crazy in lust, my heart palpitated, my blood pressure rose around him. I couldn't think straight or form full sentences. *Oh my, does he like me back?* I would think. *Yes, too sick and too respectful. Or was it too crazy to carry me along on his road to darkness and decay?* I could not figure out why he seemed so interested in me one minute and would totally ignore me the next.

I'm so glad I was not part of those last few months. All our friends who visited talked about how much weight he'd lost, how bad he looked. Why did he connect with me so dearly and then act like he didn't know me, repeatedly? Some things I'll just never know. I could not have grieved that deeply then, too much, way too much grief on my plate.

Single and Sober: Who Found My Slipper?

Was he that crazy? Was my picker that far off the mark? Was he the perfect mate or a perfect mess? Was he respecting me not bringing me into his life to become his caregiver? Or was he simply lost in his own survival world and ignoring me because I was not that important when he had his own life and death matters to contend with? Was our electricity part of my reality or just a fantasy? Or was the electricity part of his mental illness?

I thought he was my knight in shining armor, and he confirmed it when he told me the story of how he proposed to his wife on a freaking horse in Port Townsend. That's my kind of romance, okay?!? I've been looking for that fairy tale my entire life. He stole my heart, he charmed my friends, he loved my dog, he joined my home group, then he ignored me as if we'd never met. Then he died. Wow. What just happened? Look after my sister and brother, would you, Stan?

32 JOINING SANGHA – DECEMBER 2016

It was one year ago that I was drawn to go with my friend to Seattle on a Saturday to try out a Buddhist Recovery meeting. How fun! Everett rarely has cool stuff like that. I remember going to a meeting with meditation a couple times and loving it. Then there was that day retreat in Seattle where Kevin Griffin did a Dharma talk and compared the 12-Steps with Buddhism. Ha. Hundreds of recovering people showed up, the place was packed.

I thought I was unique when I compared these two items back in college in the late nineties. I had an assignment to take something I knew about, thus, the 12-Steps, and compare it with something I knew nothing about like Buddhism. I remember The Four Noble Truths and The Eightfold Path. They lined up so nicely with the 12-Step process. I never knew what to think of Buddha, though. Is he a God? A Jesus like dude? Mystical, magical, or ordinary? It seems like he was an ordinary dude who became enlightened, a wise one for certain. Not sure, but

Single and Sober: Who Found My Slipper?
I've been drawn to correlating recovery with Buddhism for the past two decades. Buddhism could complement the spiritual path I've been granted through working the 12-Steps. I am drawn to learn more.

The Buddhist Recovery meeting was inviting and worth the drive into the city. My traveling buddy and I loved the meeting and wanted to go every week. We began carpooling and going out for lunch afterward. He and I went out for a healthy Pho' soup nearby with members from the group before making the trek back home to Everett week after week. Eventually, we started to plan a sister group north of Seattle, to develop our own Buddhist Recovery Sangha, Spiritual Community, meeting in Everett and we took the action to follow through.

It turned out that the coolest church and building in Everett were talking about starting some kind of different recovery meeting in their building when I made the call. Naturally, it seemed a divine intervention was at play.

We started the Buddhist Recovery Group up north with Seattle's literature based on Using the Buddha's Teachings to Overcome Addiction on Valentine's Day 2016. The first night we had twenty-four people attend. There was such great energy, fabulous people, some experienced with Buddhism and others more familiar with the 12-Steps. Between the other facilitator and I, we knew a lot of folks from local 12-Step meetings. When they learned about this group starting up, they were excited to learn more also.

Everyone loved the environment of the Colonial building. It had huge structural columns outside that were welcoming. The comfortable living room space in the basement was inviting, too, with pretty carpet and couches. We turned the hall into our Sangha by setting out cushions, candles, and a statue of the Buddha on a low table in the middle of our circle.

We opened the meeting following a script created by earlier Buddhist Recovery facilitators. The message to begin the group is good, and the discipline is fantastic. The teachings are called the Dharma. It is fascinating and stems from ancient wisdom, teachings of the Buddha. The material we use is priceless. I love providing the community an alternate path to recovery, spiritual but not Christian, for people like me who want to explore that side of themselves.

There is such dogma in the 12-Step rooms that traditional religion, even using the word God can turn people off. These are often the very people in recovery that so desperately need love. To quiet the mind and learn from ancient teachings is essential in recovery. To harness the chatter, live with integrity, and apply loving kindness toward self and others is a goal I loved to introduce. That is attractive.

Plus, it just gives my twenty-four years of the same old, same old recovery path a facelift. I am once again rejuvenated in my journey to recover and help others.

At first, I was taking a Christian friend/sponsee with me, but she got freaked out when somcone told her there was no God in Buddhism. She interpreted that to mean this was devil worshiping in disguise. I don't see this religion as only a path for atheists because it lines up with my beliefs and I'm a believer. Some Buddhists I know include God in their practice. Especially those who learn from Kevin Griffin, Author of *One Breath at a Time* and other books.

Single and Sober: Who Found My Slipper?

This could be another option for someone to begin to believe in the power of stillness who does not currently. I don't know, maybe I'm kidding myself. I was fired as her sponsor that day. That wasn't about the, no God means you're following the Devil program, as she understood it. That was more about my sponsee being her own sponsor and not wanting to do her fourth Step.

I think mindfulness and spirituality are synonymous. To me, any religion that calls other paths devil worshiping is questionable at best and dangerous at worst. I am drawn toward love, not hate. The Buddhists encourage people to try things out and then come to their own conclusions.

Anyway, I'm on fire for my recovery again and have been for the past year. Right off the get go in December last year, maybe January, I attended an all-day retreat at the Buddhist Center that was simply amazing. It was a six-hour workshop with conversation, meditation, and enlightening insightful processes. It was so wonderful. I was stiff and nervous for sure, but it was nice to be still, to notice my thoughts, and guide them to silence.

I was chosen to become a Mitra and was indoctrinated through a sacred ceremony. I entered a training program out of Seattle, attended several three-and four-day retreats, and committed to four years of Mitra study to learn more about Buddhism. I absolutely loved deepening my friendship with the Buddhist Community and following its ideals, values, and practices. Unfortunately, I was only able to give one year of study before life got in the way.

During my first one day retreat I found it great to learn more about my body, the anxiety I experience, and witness discomfort come and go. I remember my feet falling asleep and instead of having to move, to shake it off, I focused on being still and observing. I watched the slight pain be there and leave. Hunger came and went, and then it was lunchtime. Volunteers made a delightful vegetarian soup. What a great day. I wanted more and walking afterward felt like such a luxury after sitting for so long.

Now, a year later, our Buddhist Recovery meeting continues to thrive. I was asked to save the dates of an upcoming retreat in Vancouver, Canada in mid-December. I did this. Anxious to learn more about what four days of a Buddhist Recovery retreat would entail, hoping it was not all meditation as I didn't feel prepared for that. At the most I practice fifteen minutes a day, and that can sometimes be per week. I am willing, but I need answers before I register to attend the retreat.

33 DEATH AND BUDDHISM – DECEMBER 2016

There is so much death in my life it sometimes feels overwhelming. I'm starting to gamble more. Teddy. Pain. Grief. I hate it that Teddy died. Three months now and it still hurts. Lonely, sad, such a freaking shame. Senseless. He really didn't know his addiction was so bad. He died, was brought back to life with Narcan and intubation. He lived a day to talk about it and still questioned if he needed help. "Do you really think I'd be assessed as needing inpatient treatment? Couldn't I just go to outpatient?" he asked sincerely. He died that weekend for a second time, and he isn't coming' back. This disease is so ridiculous. I love you Teddy, rest in peace my buddy, my pal, my friend.

Then my brother-in-law died a month later, suddenly and unexpectedly. My sister will never be the same. I took another trip to Michigan to be with her and help with another funeral.

The grief started when I first got into recovery, I grieved about losing my lifestyle, my friends, and the way I coped with my emotions. My mom died my first week of sobriety, my niece after that, my dad, then both siblings. Death just keeps coming up all around me. After decades in recovery, so many addicts and alcoholics have died either using or due to complications from using. I need to participate being in the moment, accepting death, and appreciate living.

While I'm away I remember the deadline to get my down payment paid if I planned to attend the four-day Buddhist Recovery Retreat in Canada. I don't have the agenda I requested, but I'm going to put it out there on faith and pay the $50 downpayment without knowing anything except the title: The Spiritual Death of an Addict. Sounds perfect.

Food, gambling, sugar, looking for love in all the wrong places. I need to let it go. The obsessions. The beating myself up. The out of integrity behaviors that are creeping in again since Teddy died. I need to get back on track. I'm going on this retreat and trusting I will be ready to sit for four days if need be or donate the registration money and stay home if it turns out I'm not ready for all that quiet when the time comes.

I returned to Washington from the second Michigan funeral and received the email stating the retreat is now full and registration is closed. What? I still don't know the agenda and they want my payment in full. Now I haven't even spread the word in our group because I don't know how to promote it with only a title. What are we to expect? It's in another country and many recovering alcoholics and addicts can't cross the US/Canadian border due to being felons. I got my passport, but it took some time and effort, and some cash. How's the group going to get to attend? Shoot. I'm really disappointed. I sent back an email stating I'm still waiting for my prior email questions to be answered and I can't believe it's closed. I asked if there was any more room.

I received a great and personal email from the facilitator of the retreat stating they've been out of the country for a three-month study and were off grid for email. They took accountability for dropping the ball. They let me know the topic, that there was no agenda, and payment in full is due by November 30. I can live with that, especially since they said if I have someone from the states that I want to travel with they'll try to make room for one more because often someone will cancel.

I am excited now. I inform my group saying I have room for one person to travel with. A lady is willing to be a backup if I don't find anyone, and she has the money to travel, share a hotel, and pay the retreat registration. I'm thrilled to try something new and scared I won't be able to talk or move for the entire four days. It's a silent meditation retreat but I still don't know what that really means.

I was grateful for the lady from the group to be a backup, which freed me to pay without regret by the time of the deadline and begin to explore hotels, maps, and time frames. No one else came forward wanting to attend. Still nervous about sitting in meditation for four days, spending money on hotels, unclear if anyone will offer to host us for a night here and there, and unsure if this possible long stretch of silence is for me. Because I'm anxious to know more about Buddhism and Recovery, I continue to trust the process.

Last weekend I drove down to Seattle's East and West Bookstore and bought a bunch of books about Buddhism. Now I have my group's book about Triratna Buddhism, a Joseph Goldstein book explaining similarities between Theravada, Tibetan and Zen Buddhism, and a couple more to explore Triratna specifically. I keep hearing terms that are foreign to me that I'm expected to understand, but I don't. As an overachiever I want to go to this retreat prepared, and an expert ha-ha. I'm such a perfectionist, a blessing and a curse. Nothing's ever perfect and I end up exhausted trying.

I was glad to get the next email explaining that I did not need to get a referral for hotels because this is a residential retreat. Oh yay. I also learned all meals are included!!! This expensive retreat just became an exceptionally good deal, and I can relax. The only thing I need to fear is fear itself. Ahhh. Exhale. Let it go.

I spent the week reading the Goldstein book and have an idea of the basics of Buddhism. I'm loving the book even more now that I have an outline of Buddhist teachings, the format of how to run a peer-based meeting, which I've already been doing, and the informative text from the facilitator which is brilliant. I felt that was the case, but now I'm really seeing it.

The Buddha was in recovery from his obsessive mind and reached enlightenment by learning to refrain from actions that cause suffering; like clinging to or avoiding things.

The spiritual principles are in alignment with the 12-Steps in letting go, living by moral values, and helping others. Maintaining the spiritual condition is key. Ha. So familiar. Buddhist teachings note "Happiness is Harnessing the Mind". Our gift to the world is based upon the following: generosity, morality, respect, service, listening to the Dharma-the teachings, meditation...these are the "Actions For Good". Yes ma'am. One Dharma. Peace. Be still.

Two weeks to go until the retreat. Bought some comfy cotton clothes that won't reveal all my newfound fat but are Buddhist Retreat appropriate and make me feel pretty. I've been turning to my friend, Little Debbie, as a source of comfort dealing with all the grief lately. I love that this retreat is December 15-18 as it's right when the rest of the world is gearing up to honor commercialism and pay tribute to the birth of Jesus by getting into debt.

I'm doing my share of spending but attempting to refrain from the insanity of the holidays this year. No tree, maybe lights, no big deal. My adult son continues to get spoiled and now I'm also sending gifts to extended family, too. I chose to focus my attention on great nieces and nephews and be generous. I won't go into debt over it, but I will not be stingy either.

I like to treat myself at this time of year, which I've already done with paying for this retreat. Love and kindness are okay. Going with it. Letting go of the fear. Non-attachment to tit for tat with gift giving. Not having the greedy desire to receive. Really, this year I want to give to myself and to others. It's okay. Happiness is not about what I get, it's about what I give and what I do.

I also want to send my sister something fabulous as she is alone having just lost her husband. Christmas is bound to be simply strange for her this year. Extra love and kindness are a must. I want to ease her burden of Christmas expectations and shop for her family, too. We'll see what the future has in store. What is available in the stores and in my bank account will predict the outcome, too.

Grief is the hardest emotion for me to walk through in my recovery without picking up something to dull the pain. My people are dying all around me. Both my parents died. My dear niece died at twenty-nine years old, suddenly, of a brain aneurysm. I am not over my big sister's death in 2012. She raised me when both parents were sick with active alcoholism. At eleven she became my guardian and at thirteen she became my legal custodian. She has forever been my sister, my confidant, and my best friend. I'm not over my big brother's death in 2013 either. He was a hippie, an activist, and a scholar. In addition to my close, lifetime friend, Teddy, and my brother-in-law dying a few months ago, four sponsee's of mine began the death process again.

Three of my current sponsee's have relapsed, all with over twenty years clean and sober, and an ex-sponsee who relapsed has died. It is hard not to want to stuff the grief, the guilt, the shame, and the lie. I feel grief as I miss them all. I feel guilt that I didn't call them out on their behavior long before they picked up. I feel shame because I'm the common denominator. Multiple people I tried to help lost their way, and I feed the lie when I tell myself I wasn't a good enough sponsor. I want to sweep the emotions under a rug.

Instead, I go to a meeting, to the four-day silent retreat, to the fellowship, and I get honest. I've learned suffering is all about averting or clinging to how things used to be. I suffer when I expect what happens in life not to change. I know this disease is deadly and all my sponsee's have made their own choices. I am fortunate that I haven't had to pick up and I appreciate the miracle every day of my life.

The pain of the grief is in direct contrast to the joy I feel being present in my life through the work I do in both the 12-Step program and through Buddhist Recovery. I don't take it for granted. Part of me dies when those around me relapse or die. The beauty is that it makes me want to live even deeper. August 10, 1992 I was born again when I stopped using substances. December 31, 1999 I stopped smoking cigarettes. Both my siblings died of lung cancer at fifty-nine years old. In December 2016 I became a Mitra, I decided to take my spiritual journey to an entirely new level. Acceptance of life and death is key.

34 TOM – JANUARY 2017

President Trump Inauguration - Protests in every city USA. The citizens of the US voted for a reality TV star to run the most powerful nation in the world. Let's see who gets fired. Hilary had more votes. I don't think I even want to understand or accept politics as they've become so insane. I breathe and pray for peace.

Life is so strange. Just when I believe I truly am loving myself, my life, and knowing I am not alone as I am part of everything and everyone in spirit and energy, I fall prey to the Plenty of Fish app I haven't deleted.

Part of me thinks someone 'out there' is going to fill me up. Most days I feel such satisfaction. I'm so full, so much a part of love and life. I know I would not be a good part of a couple as I'm so set in my ways. Then, I got a message from someone who works nearby, is close to my age, and he seems fun and stable. A storyteller who has a "good profession" who likes folk, rock, and blues music. He's traveled all over the world, and he has got to have a perspective just a little broader than the average Everett man.

At first, he offers to go for coffee and tell me a story and I am intrigued. Still, I put him off until we can chat back and forth a bit, and I can get a feel for him. Then one night when I was off work, cranked up on caffeine, and feeling a bit bold, I told him yes, he could take me for coffee and tell me a story.

We met last week for coffee. He's a lot older than his picture, but decent looking and still in his uniform from work. He is a manager for the commuter train into the city. He comes across as sharp and stable. He's been working for the transit for decades. Wow. He has the perfect end of career job doing one trip into the city and one trip back in a day's work. Nice.

I am somewhat attracted, and I like him right off, but the jury was out initially. This was due to his staring off my right shoulder when he talked to me. With only the wall behind me, it seemed odd that he didn't keep eye contact as he was born and raised in America. However, he talked in an engaging and honest way about what he thought and believed, etc.

That is where the night got interesting. He starts asking me Trump or Hillary? and I'm thinking he's kidding but he's not. He has the *make America great* slogan ready to spout at the tip of his tongue and asks me political questions that are inappropriate for a first date. Tom has serious problems with all the homeless people in Seattle, and he refuses to give money to young people unless they have a visible disability.

He doesn't have a clue about what they go through and believes they all choose to live in poverty with a sign and they need to get a job. He hates that taxpayers give money to programs that help poor people who could just make better choices.

When I talked about Schizophrenia, Bi-polar, people who are developmentally delayed, hospitals closing, the opiate epidemic, the lack of mental health and substance abuse beds he reiterated they could all go to work, make better choices, and not rely on hard working people to support them.

I don't know who he thinks is supporting them, but holding signs in freezing weather and sleeping under viaducts means we are not good supporters, for real.

But I'm calm. I am listening and not defensive. My meditation and Buddhist teachings are taking over. I have faith and I'm being kind. Even though a couple times I wasn't breathing as my anxiety kicked in and although I felt like arguing, I didn't. I was an observer, noticing and I let it slide. His belief system is not my fight and I'm not feeling defensive most of the conversation. This is amazing growth for me.

"This is really good Chinese Food" he says, and I agree. "I don't eat in Chinese restaurants where Chinese people eat because Chinese people will eat anything, sort of like animals" he proudly spews while spitting as he talks with his mouth full. He continues to shovel multiple bites into his mouth before swallowing. Tom goes on to explain how he will only eat at a Mexican Restaurant that serves Mexicans because they know authentic Mexican food. My stomach starts to churn but I'm attempting to breathe and just notice. We certainly have different beliefs.

At one point during dinner Tom talked about how fat so many people are and how they just need to do something about it. Then he explained how fat he was until he got divorced three years ago and started going to the gym and working out.

It was interesting to observe him think out loud and admit had the divorce not occurred he never would have gone to the gym or started eating better. It was clear Tom wasn't currently going to the gym, and he wasn't healthy and oblivious to the fact that he was talking about himself.

He eats meat and wants dessert, and I don't eat meat or consume sugar. He works at 4:00 am and I work the swing shift. He's Trump and I'm Hillary, possibly Bernie. I do not think we could be any more different. However, I did not want to leave immediately, and the shrimp and rice was nice as most guys barely spring for coffee until they decide if they want to continue to date. I have decided under no conditions will I go out with him again due to his conservative nature and my liberal ways. But when he asks me if I will go out with him again at the end of the dinner, I say "yes".

What the heck is that about? In my mind I am justifying it just isn't cool to say no directly. Rejection is tough. I can always say "I thought about it...decided probably not a good fit" over the phone or text. There I was giving him my number and saying yes. Why do I continue to say yes when I mean no?

I'm thinking I will give him the wrong number, I'm aware I'm about to engage in a full blown lie. Just then he says I'll call you right now and you'll have my number. Okay, I would rather speak the truth anyway. I'll wait to see if he asks me out again and then gently say no. Why can't I be direct? What is that about?

The fear outweighs my need to stand up for my truth. When will I be able to face that fear and walk through it? I've gotten better in certain circumstances, but this is where I'm still a scared little schoolgirl frozen with fear. I'm willing to sacrifice my integrity to spare him rejection. Why do I run from confrontation and avoid discomfort when I'm left feeling worse than if I told the truth? That's what makes me want to turn to food, gambling, the illusion of love, and buy a bigger rug.

I'm sick of dating, online dating, hoping for a relationship that I have lost confidence could ever come to fruition. The daydream of having a partner in recovery that is healthy and compliments me, who appreciates me and whom I reciprocate these feelings, is just a dream. To find someone who loves to work with me around the house, who loves to travel, who wants to go to concerts and play music, well I'm not convinced it even exists.

Then my friends remind me that I can't just go off to four-day meditation retreats and jump in my car and go to movies or make play dates with friends unless it all lines up with both of your desires and schedules. That's when I think I might not be comfortable with the lifestyle of being in partnership either. I guess it boils down to having freedom or being in a relationship. There is no choice for me, but I do wonder if the right partnership would have to be a choice.

Anyway, I'm going to a meeting now instead of the bakery. Life is full of choices.

35 DOMINIC – JUNE 2017

I'm thrilled to have a date today with Dominic from Plenty of Fish. I am surprised that I can still feel excitement and hopeful after so many dates from online dating sites that have not worked out. These days nobody even reads profiles. It's like distributing cards from a deck. Yes, no, or not sure. They are even color coded with green check marks or red X's on the photographs of faces and a silver not sure option. No wonder people post twenty-year-old pictures. I am looking for someone who is available and interested and I can't even begin to find that simply by swiping photographs.

I realized I'm not necessarily seeking Electric Chemistry like with Dazzling Don, come close, no, go away, type of cat and mouse insanity. Nor do I want the eager Ethan or pretty Paul kind of games. I believe that I could grow to love anyone. What I do not understand is why twenty-five years since my last significant relationship I am still without someone to love.

At this point, I want someone whom I can share the last chapter of my life. I want to go out on mystery dates and grow to love and respect my future partner. I've been to the ball. I lost my glass slipper. I know the perfectly suited man who is devoted to his spirituality will be at the center of seeking this old gal from the projects. He'll hold the mate to my glass shoe.

I do not want someone broken and it's becoming clear that wanting to share my recovery lifestyle with another in recovery is dampening my pool of healthy men. I hope whoever finds me through my lost glass slipper can accept my continued growth and participation in the fellowship. The perfect person does not have to be in recovery themself. After Don I am not excited to date anyone, but I do not want to give Don the power to stop my quest to find someone to love who is worthy and respectful.

Then Dominic sends me a message on Plenty of Fish and I'm impressed. After a few interactions he wants to take me to dinner. I am hungry and ready in more ways than he knows. He has me pick the place, he doesn't care where. This sure beats Dutch treat lattes at a coffee shop, which is more common than one might think in my online dating experiences.

Dominic is not afraid to invest, and he is willing to make a good impression. He arrives clean, shaven, in a nice dress shirt and pants, and tells me to order whatever I want. Relieved, I ordered what I wanted.

Dominic is shorter than I tend to go for, but he's healthy and in good shape. He is a great conversationalist, totally present, and values respect. The connecting moment was when we talked about online dating. I talked about how scary it is to risk rejection or rejecting someone. He totally understood and stated he usually doesn't go on a second date unless he's really interested. We are both interested, I believe, and we agree to go out again.

We have a few things in common and Dominic is new to the area. We both love food, so eating together becomes a nightly routine right off the bat. He's more active than I am even though he's six years older. I'm all about a walk and I'd love to show him around WA. Dominic is from Missouri and I'm a little worried he's a right winged gun bearing pro-lifer who would find all my friends from the fellowship to be low life's.

But after three great dates, visiting his apartment, and going to a photography class together, I still have no clue if this is my imagination and my bias because he's from the south. Also, I'm unsure if he has any judgmental attitudes at all. In fact, he talks non-stop but doesn't say a whole lot. Sure, I know he's a manager of a large group of factory workers from third world countries. They make plastic molds and send them all over the world, but I don't know how he votes. Seems weird to ask him straight up, yet I'm curious and I want to know. I need to feel something and he's so agreeable I'm not sure if he has no opinion or if he avoids conflict at all costs playing the nice guy.

As much as I despised Andy's questionnaire, I decided to play a game with Dominic to better know him. The difference is that I'm willing to play the game too. I'm eager to discuss our answers, but I'm not willing to have him answer after me because I'm sensing he's a anything you want, babe, kind of guy. While that would be an easy personality to hang out with, I would be wondering what's beneath all that fluff and never be sure how he really felt about things.

Now we are one week into our relationship, we've seen each other five times, and we are texting daily. He is wondering why I haven't told my friends about him yet. I'm feeling a little possessed since we haven't earned that bond yet, and I'm anxious to find out if we have anything more in common than not wanting to eat alone. We talk about our day's work, but my suicide clients and his plastic moldings are not clicking in the common interest's department.

I do like this guy, but he wants me to hang out and eat cornbread and beans and talk about his perfect children that are becoming doctors and such. He doesn't even know me, and I am not ready for house slippers and curlers yet. One glass slipper would be different.

Dominic invites me into his bath and bedroom to see how neat and clean they are. He explains he's about to buy a house. That's great, but I'm a month or two out from being comfortable enough to bring him into my home and I am not a fanatical house cleaner. I would prefer to visit my friends or do something creative than clean my toilet or bathtub which I will eventually get around to. My living room is usually presentable, though. Does Dominic care if my bathroom needs attention? How important is that to him? My son bought me a plaque that says, "Dog Hair, Don't Care". I wonder if he would care?

I feel him out. "Dominic, would you be willing to play a game, answer some questions and then meet & discuss them? I'll answer them, too…". He's willing, cool. He is truly a good sport. I sit and write twenty questions, half of which are light & airy, silly & fun. The other half could tell me about his political affiliation, his religious beliefs, and how open minded he is toward people who have alternative lifestyles.

After all, what would he think to know my best friend is gay, I used to be addicted to meth, and my son has a tattoo across his entire back? I fell asleep and the next day he was a little mad that I didn't send my questions that evening. Hum. That was a misunderstanding. I'm impressed he said something.

At 3:00 the next day he invites me out to dinner. We agreed to meet at 5:00. I'm literally naked at the day spa having just had a massage. I agree to meet him but need to run home, type up the twenty questions, and make myself presentable. Bam. Done. Arrive on time. Yahoo.

I chat with Dominic for twenty minutes or so, we order, and then start in on the questions. I ask him to answer them while I answer them and then we'll share our answers and discuss the ones we want to talk about. As we read the questions off my phone, I am cracking up that A) I am really doing this and B) that these questions are hilarious, and they should be fun to discuss. I feel weird for putting him on the spot, but he seems to be willing and was disappointed it didn't happen the night before.

The first question: Hard, soft, or soft and wet? (Get your mind out of the gutter, I'm talking about ice cream.)

He did not laugh and said, "soft and wet ice cream". I explained this was meant to have a sexual undertone and it was also meant as an ice breaker. He still did not smile. The pen protector in his pocket started to look different and I was wondering if he was just a nerd or nervous. I don't mind nerds, but a sense of humor does help. Perhaps that was over the top on my part. We move on.

I learned he likes rock music over country, jazz or folk which surprises me. He changed his political stance to match my answer from Jeb Bush to somewhere between Hillary and Bernie, and he stood up against his pastor to allow gay people to come to their church. He said this was because sinners need a place to worship. He would have lost me if he said Donald Trump, and he kind of lost me on the gays answer. However, he also won my respect as he was advocating in a very liberal way in his conservative atmosphere. We don't agree that being gay is a sin. I don't even believe in sin which was too deep for the conversation at this time.

I was still willing to talk and date, but after another evening I still found almost nothing to connect on. I like that he's hard working, he honors Christianity, I like that he's a believer, and he wants to and is ready to share his life with someone. I don't like that I am not feeling even a little spark with him. I'm trying to like him because he feels like a smart bet. He loves his family, he is interested and available, but I'm just not connecting. I'm thinking we must have at least some rock music favorites in common.

Then I learned about why two of his three kids don't talk to him. The way he tells it, twenty years ago he told his wife if she didn't put out then he was going to find it elsewhere. He reports to me that three years after that conversation he found the right woman to have sex with. When his wife found out he was accused of cheating, and she wanted a divorce. Dominic truly doesn't see this as cheating and believes his wife, who knew this was coming, turned his children against him. His kids are furious and two of the three have no contact with him and haven't for the past twenty years.

I was impressed that Dominic continued to pay child support for his three kids, and is proud of his devotion to them, but he is very angry his kids resent him. He has a lot of energy about this. It was the only time I saw real emotion come from him. He's in a lot of pain that his kids still don't talk to him after two decades, which I can only notice is keeping him from living.

I want to give him my 12-Step advice in having learned the benefits of taking responsibility for my part in things. If I want to find freedom, I must be accountable, ask for forgiveness, and make amends, but of course I refrain. He is not ready to hear this and not able to see his part. I have no problem not judging him for what he did twenty years ago, but I am concerned that he is unable to see how his behavior and justification has ruined his life.

The one characteristic I hung onto was his sense of respect. Now I'm seeing that he wasn't exactly respectful to his wife or kids when it mattered the most and, heck, I guess I'm judging away. I do see a flag when the people one is closest to have stopped all communication. Multiple people especially.

I am not feeling it with Dominic. Maybe I'm a prude, too picky, living in fairy taleland, but I have no desire to keep this going.

I must let Dominic down gracefully. He is a nice guy, but not for me. It is weird to break up with someone after a week. I hate rejection so much, I hate rejecting others, but I don't want to pretend to be interested in plastic molding. I am not.

Tell me about the lives of the people who work for you. What about the Vietnamese woman who cleans your toilets at work? What is her story? How about the young man from Cambodia you spoke of? Who are his parents? What are his values?

Goodbye Dominic. Glad we got to share the meals and I feel good that I paid for half, maybe I didn't leave you feeling used. I did apologize for the questionnaire, and I won't do that again to anyone. Perhaps it could be a useful tool for pre-marital counseling. When I broke it off with Dominic, I wish he hadn't thrown in the "I didn't feel it for you, either" reply. If that were true and he continued to ask me out and text me daily, I would feel used. Are we all so desperate that we'll settle for anyone just to not be alone?

I'd rather be alone. Thank you, God, for my pets that think I'm all that and a bag of treats. Especially when I bring them some.

36 COVID CARL – MARCH 2020

I've been dating less and less and not missing it. I love to go out to dinner and long for male companionship. However, I have been taking myself out to dinner, to the movies, and to a meeting alone, and having fun. I also go out with friends and acquaintances from the fellowship(s), especially my current best friend, my sponsor, and our Step study friends.

I'm excited when one of my friends in the program calls and says she's got a brother-in-law that she thinks I'll really connect with. Seems he is Buddhist and she's been wanting to set us up for a long time. I am willing to let her give out my number and I wonder if Carl will call or not.

I'm pleasantly surprised when he calls right away. We talk and he seems pleasant. We do have a few things in common. He is conscious of what he eats, active in his Buddhist practice, and loves to meditate. Well heck, I think this sounds attractive to me! We set up a time to meet on the weekend and decided to meet at a health food café in downtown Everett. Perfect, it's right across from the Art Gallery. I'm thinking maybe we could go for a walk after lunch and stroll through the gallery.

I am drawn to him immediately. He's tall, kind, and a gentleman. We have lunch, laugh, and the conversation is easy and effortless. He tells me a bit about his Buddhist tradition, and I share a little about mine. I leave out some of the recovery focus until I know if he's addict in recovery friendly. We took a tour of the art gallery afterward and still want to hang out. He offered to show me his dance studio a few blocks away.

At this point I'd heard about a local nursing home where a few of the residents died of some kind of flu, a Corona Virus they were calling it. I'd heard that it started in China and just hit the states. Some of the places around town that served elderly people, like this dance studio, closed down for fear of spreading the bug. I thought it was a bit extreme, really, but I was open to learning more. The trip to the dance studio was a bust as the doors were locked until further notice.

Neither of us were ready to part yet, it had only been a two-hour date and we were still having fun. We were holding hands and grinning and enjoying each other's company. We decided to go see a movie. Finding out we were an hour early for the next showing I walked with him to a little Chinese Restaurant nearby for some tea. Again, we snuggle up on the same side of the booth and it feels terrific. We walk back to the theater, finish off the date with a movie, a sweet drama, a good kiss, and call it a night.

The next day I'm still enamored about having such a nice and casual date, it was very natural, so easy. Then I started thinking about getting with Carl the following weekend like we arranged, and I began to get scared. It was not about being afraid to move forward with romance. I was eager for that. I started to put some pieces together about his Buddhist practice, looked it up, and found he didn't know a thing about it. We talked nightly during the week, and I didn't find much depth intellectually or emotionally. I began to question that first date. Was I seeing a mentally, physically, and spiritually fit man because that's what I wanted to see? I began to doubt my initial perception.

As the week unfolded and my anxiety increased, I realized I was not alone. It seems a global pandemic was happening and businesses all over the world were shutting down. Driving through Everett to work was a ghost town. Mine was the only car on the road. Everyone was being sent home. It was especially true for those of us older folks and in high-risk health categories that involved respiratory illnesses. I have had my lung collapse twice and I'm now sixty. I am scared for my life.

The clincher for me was that he was sick during our date and sick all week when we spoke on the phone. Carl minimized the runny nose and cough, the mild fever and congestion as simply a cold.

I just couldn't go through with our date as planned. Not only was every place in town closed or closing, but I could not see myself holding his hand or kissing him as we'd talked about. I was frozen in fear that he had the virus and would give it to me. I would probably die if I got it, my lungs are the weakest part of my body after two lung collapses in my past. I was hospitalized and needed a chest tube in both instances.

I let him know I could not move forward in a relationship at this time. I was kind and gentle, but honest.

He was hurt. He sent me a nasty text. It showed his dark side. I was right about his spiritual practice being non-existent if that text was an indicator. A few days later he apologized and asked if I would reconsider. Thank you, but no. Standing firm. Be well. These were the scariest of times.

37 GEOFF – MARCH 2022

Geoff from Mindful.com is sixty-five. I'm sixty-two now and growing older every day. He's hot stuff, especially on paper. He reaches out to me. Perfect match. Buddhist, almost three decades in recovery. He's good looking and meditates daily, making him even more attractive. He's looking for a partner who shares his spiritual path. He does yoga, meditation, and silent retreats. He starts and facilitates 12-Step groups and Buddhist meetings. I can't believe he is also a psychotherapist. Are you kidding? We have the same credentials and are at the same place in our lives. I am now working as a Behavioral Health Specialist providing psychotherapy to low-income patients without insurance or on Medicaid or Medicare. I may have met my match!

Geoff asked me for my phone number after a few chats from the Mindful.com dating site. I'm so elated. I need a happy forever after ending for my life, and for my book. We talked for an hour. There is electricity and so much of a common lifestyle. We both need to hang up but we each keep talking. The endless questions, the feel-good hormones. It's there, a connection. Yay. I'm so thrilled. Could he be the one I've waited thirty years to meet?

He was just getting ready to leave for a ten-day silent retreat. I have so many questions and a desire to know him better. From my own three and four-day silent retreats, I know it's hard to return to the real world. I give him space. He doesn't call but he does text a couple times. I'm craving him, wanting to keep the energy alive, but he's reluctant. I don't know why, but he's slow in responding to messages and not calling. He takes two days to respond to a text. No calls. I wonder what's up with him.

After five days of not hearing from him, I put myself out there. "I am ready to talk, text, or email if you are still interested, let me know. I really like you and want to get to know you better."

A day and a half later he responded that he is still interested, just busy. He invited me to his home group on zoom and offered to send me the link. Wow. Going to someone's home group is like meeting their family. He also said maybe we could talk over the weekend. I agreed to both the meeting and talking on the phone over the weekend. I decided I would leave work early to attend his home group for starters, but then he never sent the link until I reminded him ten minutes before the meeting started.

I was able to log on to Zoom and join the meeting. Ahh it all came back to me. The best parts of this recovery meeting were at my fingertips, and I did not have to be sidetracked and caught up in facilitating this Buddhist Recovery meeting like when I led the meeting in Everett. Our local group had to shut down during COVID.

Attending Geoff's meeting I had no pressure to keep

the doors open or be involved in the politics of the business end. No setting it up, tearing it down, just clicking a link and being with other like-minded people.

Wouldn't you know a reading out of Kevin Griffin's book "One Breath at a Time" is the topic. I've read the book, met the author, and found him to be a teacher and author who presents the Dharma from a place I can relate. Kevin uses a 12-Step model and Buddhism together; this is my passion.

As the meeting opens, I listen to the Four Noble Truths and the Eightfold Path. I remember why I was so drawn to these teachings. I hear people in recovery who share the desire to stop and stay stopped from different habits. Everyone was supportive of one another as we got another day under our belts. (Another day under our belts, I wonder where that expression comes from?) Geoff is the facilitator and I'm just so thrilled to see him, watch him in action, and be present in this moment. The people are terrific, very warm and inviting. The participants have various levels of experience with the Dharma and the 12-Steps. I'm home, freaking home.

The next three days are my weekend. I get no text, no call. Where is his mind? Why the prolonged responses? Why are the words and actions not in sync? Yes, I could pick up the phone, but I did that with Ethan. I pushed him and he wasn't into me. I decided not to phone or text this week and see if Geoff reaches out. Nothing. Very disappointing. Something is off and I do not know why.

I make it a point to attend this week's home group again. Someone else was facilitating. I was surprised to see Geoff join in at half time, he probably had a late-night client. I was hoping for a private chat, a word, a smile, a nod. Nothing. Maybe I was given a nod after I shared. I stuck around after the meeting ended, but still nothing personal and no clues of where he stood.

It's now twenty-four hours later and still no call, no texts. These are the most frustrating times. As Tom Petty would sing, "The waiting is the hardest part". I don't know who he is or how he thinks. I do know I'm attracted to him, and we have so much in common. I don't know what I don't know, and I can't make him want me. I have an urge to use those cheap flirtatious ways of flipping my hair, sending off those feminine pheromones, etc., but I get the feeling he's only going to notice the craving, and let it pass. Everything changes. Everything is impermanent.

Does this mean we don't live in the moment? Feel it when it's there, act on it? Maybe not. Impulsivity is usually short term. I can read too much into this silence and there is a good chance it has nothing to do with me. I will pay attention, notice, and contact him with my correct email.

Now it's the month of May, two months since we started communicating. I texted him about being on the group email list and he responded five hours later confirming the email and asking if we could talk later tonight, at 7:30. Cool, I think. I'm excited. I wait to take nerve pain medicine for my hip that makes me drowsy. I watch stupid TV to kill time. I set the alarm on my phone, so I don't drift off. I write out some questions I want to know about him, so I don't get stuck on talking all about me again. That last hour seems to drag. At 7:30 nothing. At 7:38 I get a text, "Is 8:00 ok? I'm watching the game", he writes. Yeah, no problem, I responded.

He is like clockwork, at 8:00 he calls. Again, we

chatted for 1 hour, and it went well. At 9:00, he must wrap it up. So much like psychotherapy for a 60-minute hour in the sense of the structure. This is our bi-weekly hour session, sort of. Only the context is two-way, personal, and rich. It was a little too structured, but I still find it to be very nice.

I want to know about him, but somehow, we get off talking about me again. My kitchen remodel, the glitches, the progress. Okay, now, what about you? Who are you; the recovery group facilitator, Buddhist, Counselor, and all-around Zen kind of guy?

The following week we set up another 8:00 call. I have my questions prepped. What's your experience with Buddhism? What's your recovery story? What inspired you to start this specialized group? I hope you don't mind that I shared the link with other recovering people from my area. What are you looking for in a relationship?

Notes in hand, I answer the call. I can't believe I'm tracking our conversation like I'm seeing a patient. "We corked the floor" he talks about moving into his condo five years ago. What does that mean? We. Could mean he and his brother, he and his lover, let it go Karen. He says, "I'm not a handyman…", he could have hired out, too. Darn. He's not a handyperson. Me either. I can be present for another's deepest, darkest secrets, but I just cannot crawl under the house to fix a broken water pipe.

On a side note, my friend was setting up my ice maker, broke the water pipe, and she and another friend took turns going into my crawl space to fix it. Even though it was recently cleaned and re-insulated, and without any sign of critters, I would probably drink poison rather than go under the house. It sounds like Geoff wouldn't do this either. I made a mental note. If we ever lived together, we'd have to hire a handyperson.

Geoff's experience with Buddhism was life changing for him. What a wonderful way to begin one's recovery journey! He explained how he connected the Buddhist teachings with his 12-Step background, and I simply could not believe another soul on earth had such a similar path to my own.

Now I'm embarrassed about our last conversation when he realized I was at the Buddhist Recovery Summit in 2017, that he also attended. It was one of the highlights of my life as many of my recovery and spiritual teachers were the presenters. They were my gurus at that time.

Our last conversation I was bragging about having sat next to one of my idols and had lunch with him during the Summit. Here he trained under the same man and learned to facilitate the trainers' style of recovery group from him. I didn't shut up long enough to hear this during our last conversation. I continued to mispronounce the teacher I studied under for a year, throw out names of people Geoff actually knew, and I only knew of, and I'm certain I sounded more like some name dropper than my authentic self. When I am nervous, I tend to ramble.

When I lct Geoff know I sent the zoom link to some local people interested in attending the Buddhist 12-Step group online, he said he and Leah (another facilitator) would send me $10 for each person who attended. That made me laugh, but I did confirm he was in fact joking, of course. There is no dana or donations collected, there are no kickbacks as it would go against the Buddhist principles. It went without saying. We share a similar sense of humor and language. We can donate to a sangha

Single and Sober: Who Found My Slipper?
or 12-Step group of our choice, but this online group is not even collecting dana at this time.

I want to address the question, what are you looking for in a relationship, but I chicken out. I'm going to settle for chalking up another good conversation and leave it at that. Let's just see where this leads, if anywhere. I learned he has never been married and has no kids. I have not told him about my thirty-year process of not being in a significant relationship, having never been married, but he knows I have a thirty-one-year-old male child. With that comes an assumption I was married.

Nope, I was given a promise ring that he would promise to commit. Never got the commitment and God is good. I see now that Chase was not my forever after. Neither were the bazillions of men I've met since; I am certain of this fact. It is not for lack of trying.

I do believe my higher power is guiding this process. This is true whether I'm meant to be single forever, or I haven't met the right one. Up until now? I'm such a die-hard, my will, kind of gimmie gimmie gimmie the hot dude kind of gal. I plan to let go and surrender my will. I am praying for God's will in my life and the power to carry it out. I could have had a horrible life if I followed my will in my drug using, drunken, wild, ego driven younger days. I have no regrets.

Instead, my life has been full of fun, free to be me, to come and go as I please kind of days. Although at times I am lonely and bored. I can live with that, but the idea of sharing my life with someone kind and like-minded, well it could be special. I don't want to rule it out.

The problem I have is believing the Disney based Cinderella kind of fairytale image of happily ever after will come true when I know it doesn't exist. Somehow, I still chase the proposal on a Black Stallion, the slipper that fits. The prince charming who sweeps me off my feet. Gosh, Karen, stop it. The man who meditates and is at peace with himself and the world. That's attractive.

Yet here I am chatting with a man who is a mirror image of myself. Same kind of clean time, same drug of choice, the same exact career, and traveling on this small niche spiritual path. I can't give up the dream, the fairytale, the hope.

In my twenties I would seek a man who I could find at a car wash. That meant he had a car and he washed it. My standards have changed now. I seek a man who does Yoga and has a spiritually based life. Someone who has some barometer to notice when he's out of alignment with a higher power's will. That is most desirable to me.

I have that and I seek that. The man in spandex doing Yoga is cute, but gets less cute with age, ha-ha. Who am I to talk when I have wrinkled skin and hip and back pain? I'm feeling like the humpback Grinch looking for the pretty and younger Prince Charming. Said Prince would see beyond my humps to notice the beauty I hold inside my loving heart. Guess I've got to be willing to notice the loving spirit of my next partner, despite warts and farts. Not to say Geoff has warts, but he may fart. If he has warts, I'd get used to them. I got to go now, I'm late for my home group.

Now it is June, three months since he first reached out and we still haven't met. I keep attending Geoff's home group every week and anticipate seeing him. I learned he went on another retreat, this time only four days. I love that about him. He is spending retirement how

I would like to. The other group leader, Leah, is a down to earth recovering alcoholic, friendly, organized, cute. I wonder if they are a couple.

Leah runs the next month of meetings. Geoff is in the zoom meeting eating or so relaxed it's hard to tell if he's present. At first, I sent him some personal chats, but no response during the groups. I sent Geoff a text when he missed one of the groups and learned he was on retreat. I begin to have new thoughts.

I've put myself out there a bunch now, he's not responding. I believe it's clear I'm into you. Why are you acting like I don't exist? This reminds me of Ethan. I pushed. He went for it, but I was the one pushing and, in the end, he wasn't into me. I need to back off. Let go of expectations. See if he pursues me.

Leah is looking for someone to kayak with at an upcoming event. I think, hey that might be fun. I have a couple kayaks and could get to know the group members better by attending. I could find out more about Leah and Geoff's relationship and maybe even meet him, too. I reach out to Leah, and we exchange numbers.

I don't have to assume Geoff and Leah are a couple, nor do I have to be blind. I continue to make plans with Leah until this week when a horrific rainstorm heads our way and I bow out of the event. I can't kayak in rough waters, and certainly not in the rain.

I realize the group participants are still going to the festival but focusing on checking out the covered activities rather than kayaking. If it weren't for the three or four-hour round trip, most of which is past my bedtime, I would go. The icing on the cake for me was when my local friend that was going to go with me came down with covid and had to cancel. I would have liked to help celebrate one of the group members' first recovery birthdays, though. That is always so special. Underneath all these logical reasons for not going, I was still wishing I could meet Geoff. My feelings started out electrified and have been slowly waning.

I attended the group again this week and after the meeting let Leah know for certain I would not be able to come the next day to the event. She understood. I was surprised when Geoff popped up and said with all earnestness, I am sorry you won't be able to come, I was looking forward to meeting you.

What?! Really?!! WOW. Your actions don't show that when you do not reach out and now you give me a bone. Jeez, had I known that I would have probably driven alone and gotten drenched to meet you.

Why is it so hard for either of us to ask to meet for coffee halfway between us? When or should I make that move? I'm just not feeling that he's into me.

In the meantime, I am back to practicing meditation daily. I'm enjoying the topics, the group members, and the welcoming environment that includes both Buddhist and 12-Step practices. I absolutely love that God is part of this process. It was not the norm in my history with the Tradition I studied to have room for both Buddha and God. I didn't realize when I met the leaders at the summit in 2017 that what they were offering as an option in practice was so profound and rare, even within this specialized niche of Buddhism and Recovery.

I share my unedited, unfinished book with my sister. She is excited that I've been communicating with Geoff and wants to know the details. I share an overview and for some reason I can't find the first text. I know he contacted me, but only my text is showing up as the first one. I'm beginning to believe that maybe he only sent a 'like' to me four years ago when he joined Mindful.com and was new to the area. I could have reached out to him first recently, and he's not really seeking a relationship for whatever reason anymore.

It is so weird that all the weekly group emails come from Geoff and Leah. While I know they co-facilitate the group, they are clearly in different locations. She is the forty-something version of a hippie, background filled with tasteful nick-nacks and books in an old kitchen setting. Geoff's in a modern condominium with sparse walls and fine lines. It's hard to tell where he's coming from as I seldom see a facial expression when people in the group are being funny or sad.

There is a possibility that he has become the observer, not allowing himself to go to extreme emotion, just neutral. While not getting too high or low based on other's behaviors is healthy, I haven't yet figured out if being neutral keeps a person from being a participant in life. Observing is being mindful, in the moment. This is different than being active, I think. I suppose when one is not driven by habit, lust, or impulse it would be harder to show emotion simply by being an observer.

I'm unsure if Geoff is interested in me, if he's available, or anymore I question if I'm still attracted to him. Time is my friend when I let the initial adrenaline pass to see what happens next.

Now it's February 2023. I'm still attending the online Group when I'm not doing service for another fellowship or stuck late at work. I have spent a year relearning what I forgot and being introduced to more dharma. The group continues to be small, but the members are close.

I have figured out that Leah and Geoff are not a couple. Leah started into a new relationship and is having the time of her life. Geoff has been picking up the slack and facilitating more groups as Leah travels around with her new friend.

I like Geoff, but I doubt we'd make an ideal couple. We do have so much in common, but it'd be difficult to make it work from living hours apart. He seems to be set in his ways, as am I. The spark cooled down and I'm able to form sentences now, sometimes, and simply be a group participant. I love the thirty-minute meditation, the great readings, and the short, but wise sharing.

My meditation has increased nearly to daily practice as I'm drawn to the stillness, the guided meditations, and the Dharma talks by so many of the teachers introduced in the group through audio recordings. My spirituality has expanded. It helps me guide others in Mindfulness practices both in my work as a Behavioral Health Specialist in Primary/Integrated Healthcare, and in sponsoring women in my 12-Step work.

I am content as is. The Labrador I had for thirteen years passed away. I've attempted to replace her with a terrier mix rescue and a Papillon puppy. They are my companions these days. Occasionally my grand kitty, the spectacular Savannah Leonardo DaVinci who rules the community, gets to visit with us, too. We have extremely exciting sleepovers, and I can never get enough photographs!

It's now November 2023. I continued to attend the

online meeting for twenty-months but the relationship with Geoff never took off. We never even met in person. Other obligations kept me from attending the group very often. My interest in Geoff and in the group faded as a result.

However, my daily meditation practice has become a habit again. For this I am eternally grateful. Thank you, Geoff and Leah. Peace. All is well.

38 MIKE – JUNE 2022

Last weekend I took my son out to a comedy show in Seattle. The comic, Cash Levy, was picking on the audience about what kind of jobs they do. He asked the couple sitting up front what work they did, and both answered they were doctors. Oh, where did you meet?, he asked. She blushes and spills that they met through EliteSingles.com. They'd been together for two years. Hmm. Maybe that's a sign, I thought. Get out of the way and let the miracle happen.

EliteSingles.com. There I am the following Monday signing up. I chose the one-month option for $50 versus the multi-month option for less each month. It's either going to happen or not.

I send out ten likes before I even get my profile approved. I start getting likes back, thus, making a match, and receiving messages. How cool, at it again.

Wow, what would it be like to date a normal guy? Is a normal man found on Elite.com? Do they consider themselves elite? I am not interested in a guy who is addicted unless they're clean and sober. Nor one who is abusive. Not one who needs you to pay his rent or do his laundry. Hmm, are my expectations off?

Cooking and cleaning are normal expectation of females in this world still as far as I know. Maybe he cooks and cleans too. Hey, hey. That would be the kind of normal guy I would do flips for. Mental flips, not physical ones anymore. I received messages from both Cord and Mike. Cord straight up asks me for my phone number. I go ahead and give it out, though I know nothing about him.

Mike sent me this lengthy, but beautiful and personalized message. Whoa. You don't see that often on these sites. It's usually a smile, a hi, or a mysterious match of your personality as defined by the company you paid to send you daily leads. Mike is thoughtful, spiritual, and detailed. He is so impressed by my profile that he opens up on a first message to tell me about himself and inquiries about me. We share the spiritual path of Buddhism and he's drawn to nature, too, loving animals and camping and such.

Now I am about to go to my campground to set up for the summer. I'm scared that I'll hook up the water incorrectly in my RV and bypass the hot water system or blow out the pump. I'm so lost since my best friend moved to Hawaii a few months ago. We have been hanging out almost daily for the past five years. I'm really missing her. She knew all these things. She taught me how to build a fire. I'm just saying that Mike starts looking more attractive since I bet he knows how to go glamping.

I respond to Mike and feel like I'm double dating knowing that Cord is about to call. I guess it's okay and one is expected to double or triple date when they are on these sites until and unless a match is made. Like having a coffee date for starters. I am attracted to Mike in a more authentic way than Cord. Though Cord is by far cuter and that's all I know about him.

Mike's profile has pictures of himself in the 1970's which is always weird, but his main picture is current and he's old. He's seventy-one, I'm now sixty-two. We are both old. I can't rule that out. I do want to explain why my profile says I'm 63, but I refrain. (I always use an April fool's birth date online; it makes me older than I really am for ½ the year. I don't want to give personal details to strangers.) I keep conversing. Mike seems genuine and sweet.

Then I got a message from Elite Singles that Dylan was found to be a fraud and had attempted to contact me. His profile has been deleted and there is no need to worry unless you gave him bank information.

Who is Dylan? Good thing he's not Mike or Cord. I'm glad they are legit. Good thing EliteSingles is doing something about their phishers.

Elite Singles is everything I do not like about this world and something I need because my picker is broken. I do not like educated people and people with money who think they are elite, like they are better than other people. I do not want to think of myself as a cut above the rest. I'm just another human on this earth used as a vehicle to help others keep their heads afloat, to spread compassion and love.

I hate people that think their hard work is the only thing that got them ahead in life. I know a lot of diligent workers that were not born into privilege that will never be able to pull themselves up by their bootstraps. There is no equal access due to the color of their skin, their immigration status, or their inability to focus on college when they must survive and keep their family alive as a priority. Intergenerational wealth has not been equally distributed, making the playing fields unfair.

It is difficult for me to think I deserve to have a partner who has means. I have spent my life working two jobs and going to college for eight years in order to feed my son and eventually get ahead. I don't want to live paycheck to paycheck ever again. I do not seek a partner who is going to take care of me, only one who I don't have to take care of financially, emotionally, physically, or spiritually, if I can help it. Perhaps I'm too prideful.

Wouldn't it be nice to have a grown-up, mature, capable, healthy adult to share a life with that isn't the fat old dude with a wife beater t-shirt holding up some gross fish? I would make a commitment "in sickness and in health", but I hate the idea of starting off with a sick person and taking on the role of caregiver. Down the line I believe I would do the right thing with my partner. I'm not so sure about taking on that role from the get-go. Mutuality, commonality, and two grownups both contributing and supporting one another. Is that too much to want?

Am I kidding myself that the fantasy of equal partnership, devotion, investment and matched romance even exists? At least to pretend this on a first date?!

What about the need to be right overruling every discussion from them? From me? What about the tit-for-tat stuff that interferes with daily life? Ahh, the ego that prevents the sunlight of the spirit from shining. Karen, you live in this fantasy land that you'll be happy when you meet and marry Mr. Right. Ha-ha. What about freaking just being happy now? As is!

Alone with my higher power, my two dogs, my

Grand kitty and my son nearby. I'm cool with that. I'm feeling content with myself. Sure, a little lonely sometimes, but not alone. I have my faith. I'm learning wisdom like the Buddha Dharma and the 12-Steps offer. Friends. Acquaintances. Maybe I have everything a girl needs right here and now. Hmm. Ponder that, Karen.

Dang. Another notice from Elite Singles. Cord was found to be a fraud and had attempted to contact me. His profile has been deleted and no need to worry unless you gave him bank information.

Oh, that's who was sending me text messages, "Good Morning, Karen" and the like that I never responded to because they were from numbers not in my contacts. That was close. At least I never fell for that gorgeous hunk or sent him any money.

Mike's messages are getting weird. He's into Native American art, but he's not Native and sells it to make ends meet. He's referring to the old days when he had "disposable income", meaning he's broke now. I will be too when I'm seventy-one most likely, social security isn't much to live on. I've done some planning, so I hope not to be too stifled.

This is not a deal breaker, but I'm not interested in panicking when my car breaks down or when I get a flat tire. I want to be Elite in the sense that I can afford AAA, tires, and an occasional tune up. I want to be with someone who can also afford to get past the survival mode and live out their days with their head above water.

Maybe I have become a snooty Elite single. I'm justifying turning into one of those people I've been known to despise. Picky, picky, picky. Eeewww. I just want a normal partner, but my normal has changed. As

Single and Sober: Who Found My Slipper?

Phil Ochs used to sing, "Ah but I've grown older and wiser / and that's why I'm turning you in / So love me, love me, love me, I'm a liberal".

The clincher ouch I got from Mike's messages was his referring to SS multiple times. It wasn't a reference to Social Security, I could tell by the context. I asked, what was the SS reference? Silver Singles he responds. No kidding. Now that I'm a SS he would say. Humm. I do not ever want to refer to myself as that. It sounds like a death sentence. A withered up old hag. No Siree Bob. Don't let me become a Silver Single.

Yes, my hip hurts and my bones creek. However, I am not doomed to be societies cast away heading for a home for the demented. No. Not attractive on the dating site, either. I'm not wanting to date or to be a Silver Single. Yes, I dye my hair and I'm in denial. It's my comfort zone. Stay out.

Mike has been contacting me for a month. I decided that it's my issue with the Silver Single language. Eventually, I concede to being an elder, an old fart. It just shocked me how often he referenced the SS. I think of Silver Sneaker, our local free YMCA workout program for Seniors. I probably qualify, or I will when I get on Medicare in two years, but I'm much more comfortable not working out at this moment in my life. That changes with the wind.

Mike references his mentors and teachers in practice, and I listen to some of their teachings, and it is in alignment with my faith. It is Sufi, not Buddhism, but closely related. I'm interested again and agreed to meet for coffee.

As our schedules begin to line up and we are about

to refine the details, he gets sick with respiratory problems and wants to put it off until next week. Okay, great, I don't want to get covid, I've avoided it for two and a half years, let's keep it that way. Later, I learned he did not have it, but better safe than sorry. This week we were going to meet when he traveled up north for another reason. He lives thirty minutes south of me. Cool, I can do that easily since I took a weeklong staycation from work and have time to be flexible.

Only Mike contacted me to say that he had a medical emergency and couldn't meet as planned. He was in the hospital. Okay, now that's a good reason to cancel. I am starting to wonder if he's out of the country, though. He was annoyed that he was taken to The Everett Hospital, which everyone locally knows as Providence. I was unclear if he was more familiar with Swedish Hospital down by his home or if he were looking up the area on a global map and just made up the name of what the hospital could be called.

Luckily, he was discharged after a couple of days, and he invited me to have coffee or lunch with him today. I agreed and by golly we finally met for lunch at a great little restaurant I selected halfway between our houses. The homemade soups and pastries, breads, and delightful menu at The Sister's Restaurant was something to be excited about even if the date didn't work out.

In re-reading Mike's profile, I was quite impressed as I got ready for our date. I got up early and left the campground I'm staying at and dressed nicely. Michael's profile describes him as introverted, intelligent, a reader, a lover of non-traditional faith, and humor.

He was funny when he responded to my suggestion

of meeting in Everett. I'll just refuse to be discharged, and we can eat the tremendous gourmet food I've been getting here he tells me referring to the hospital food.

I knew then we shared a sense of humor, the dry, quick one-liners. I intentionally drank an extra dose of caffeine knowing my extraverted personality can use a kicker if he's an introvert. I made a mental note to ask him about what he likes to read and to learn more about how he practices his faith. I head out to one of my favorite AA meetings prior to meeting him as it always puts me in a good mood and feeling right sized. I set the ego aside, ready to be in the moment.

I arrived wearing black pants, cute black sandals, and a new white shirt. It was long sleeved, but light weight as the sun was finally coming out at noon as I expected in typical Seattle style in the summer. I get there early enough to walk my dogs, finish my iced chai tea latte, and show up only a few minutes early. This is an improvement from my drinking days when I would intentionally show up fashionably late, often extremely late. It's such a selfish disease.

Mike is easy to spot and looks just like his photograph. Immediately I noticed his speech and gate are off and I think, he's had a stroke. He is shaken, anxious, and refers to the thick traffic on Broadway, the main thoroughfare through the north end of Everett. He used his vehicle navigation system to find the place and reports not being good at using it. Well, I understand it's difficult for a lot of us, especially old people. It took me a while to use it and even longer to trust it, which continues to be a work in progress.

We go in and order. I am giving him a chance to buy

my meal and he does not step up to the plate. I size him up. He is wearing a corduroy jacket over a T-shirt and blue jeans with plastic shoes. This is lunch, the jacket showed an effort at getting dressed up. Sweet. Corduroy is my kind of style, though it's supposed to be a hot day.

We sit down and talk. He's got a lot of ailments. He identifies with being arthritic, the rheumatoid kind. Mike said he's had an auto-immune disease since his twenties. Ahh, the speech issue is not from a stroke. All these things don't dissuade me. He's attractive, intelligent, and personable. No deal breakers. He seems like a nice guy, genuine.

Then, he talks about his auto-immune disease-causing depression. I get the distinct impression that he is untreated and rationalizes this different type of depression being studied by the scientists as being linked to the auto-immune issue. This is my area of expertise, and I must refrain from being a know-it-all and judgmental. I can't get myself to ask about antidepressants and therapy. I'm fairly sure I got the picture. He's justifying why he has depression and probably not addressing it. Just a guess. People are okay with having a dozen diagnoses, but refuse to accept a brain disorder, there's too much stigma.

I work in health care and with people suffering from depression along with other health issues every day. Naturally, if you have a chronic and debilitating illness, you are going to suffer from depression. I'm all about the solution: antidepressants and talk therapy. I've listened to people in recovery rooms insist nobody ever take an antidepressant and I think, are you going to be responsible for their suicide? Mental Illness still gets such a bad rap.

In listening to Mike, I hear him consider his

depression unique and not caused by the chemicals in his brain being off or enhanced by his living conditions. I hear him not wanting to be considered to have a mental illness and that means it is likely to be untreated. It is hard to sit back and let people go through their own process of coming to grips with their disease. Seventy percent of alcoholics have depression, too, but some choose to die by suicide instead of treating it with a benign but essential pill and counseling.

Since Mike's marriages ended, widowed once and divorced about five years ago, Mike moved into senior housing. He lives in a studio apartment he intended on staying at temporarily. He just hasn't gotten around to moving. He adds, I live like a monk. All those beautiful online photos from his backyard are photos of their last house.

Wow, he is kind of sad. Plastic shoes, a limp, funky speech, the autoimmune disease…none of these are deal breakers. Even living in a studio apt like a monk. I can deal with that.

Untreated depression, no way. I cannot allow myself to be around that life sucking disease. I have that disease too and the only thing that allows me to function are antidepressants and therapy/aka support groups and self-help preferably daily. Faith is important too if I intend on growing. Growing old, growing happy. Living happy, joyous, and free.

Then there is the day-trading passion. I didn't even respond to that. I know it's gambling and I'm susceptible to being swayed into that lifestyle again. I now have four years clean in Gamblers Anonymous, my GA sponsor, and my GA friends. This could be another deal breaker but my jury is out.

During the date and walking my dogs afterward, I am still interested in him. I know there are some flags, but I also like the person who worked as a manager for commercial insurance all his life. I am interested in the person who was so enthusiastic about bicycling that he rode his bike across America by himself. His only regret was doing it alone. I am intrigued by his focus on Sufi studies and weeklong silent retreats. He is a man of character from what I can tell. I need to stop ruling everybody out.

As we walked past the recovery café, I ran into a friend from Narcotics Anonymous who is so proud to be working there as a recovery coach. She is super friendly and wants to hug me and offers to hug him. She should honor my anonymity but doesn't. Mike knows I'm in recovery, but he is visibly taken back by running into her and being asked for a hug. He does accept the hug and then blurts out, does anybody have the time? I need to make a phone call.

As we walk back to my car, he explains that he needs to get a hold of his rheumatologist. Wow. That is sad that he is so identified as sick that he can't take the time to be in the moment. Finish the date. He's done now, back to being sick.

As I process this date, I realize that I cannot start a relationship with him. I had agreed to see him again, and I meant it this time. He said he'd like to do this again, too. Only I am not excited. He is not a happy guy. He is suffering, and I do not want him to be my project to fix. He's just waiting to get sicker and die. I would hate to be in that place. I won't say I'll never be there, I'm just not there right now.

Believe me, if I were only looking out for my unmet needs, I would go for it. He would be someone who could use a home, help at the campground, probably pay rent to me, and help a bit in the yard and/or with the dogs. I really need this bonus from a partner. He's not got too much stuff. But the sadness can stop me in my tracks. I would start out pitying him and end up pitying me. No way, Jose.

The final tidbit of information I find amusing is that he is not enrolled in EliteSingles.com. His platform is called Silver Seniors. Ha-ha, it's not a retirement home, it's the freaking dating site where he found me. Why or how he can respond to me on the Elite Singles site is beyond me. I noticed they cost the same, maybe it's to deceive members into thinking there is more of a pool to choose from. He said he's had a lot of trouble using the Silver Singles site. No wonder! Ugg.

Now I have to figure out how to say, nice to meet you, thanks, but no thanks. Oh, I hate that part. He might beat me to it, too. He was all too obvious when we met to size me up and down and I do not think he was impressed. My fifty-pound weight gain over the past decade trudging through death and depression myself has made me self-conscious, but I thought for sure my charming personality would balance to win him over. I'm not convinced there was a spark on either side, so maybe it's all good and he's relieved he didn't waste his limited money on my lunch. I guess we'll see. Mike took the news well. At least his smiley face response made me think so.

39 BILLY – JULY 2022

Billy and I met through Elite Singles. He and I texted back and forth and had a nice time bantering. There was absolutely a connection right away. Within a week we decided to meet. He lives an hour North in a lovely area on Rosario Beach and away from the crowded city life.

I was following his lead about meeting for dinner one night. Since he hadn't suggested a restaurant, I looked up a spot that seemed like a half an hour from each of us and offered a suggestion.

"You're asking me out?", he asked, impressed and repeating his delight several times. I wasn't, but I went along with the sentiment. I could afford dinner for two, there was a clear connection between us, and it'd make for a great story to tell our grandchildren. Next year, ha-ha, he was old too. I'm sixty-two now, he's the same.

He made a few restaurant suggestions, too, a bit closer to him. Okay, fine. I got to choose from the Train Wreck Bar & Grill, Wendy's fast food, or Mexican. Since I'd recently eaten Mexican, I voted for the bar/restaurant next to the Railroad Tracks up in Burlington. It had a nice menu.

Unfortunately, it was the hottest day of the year so far and the place had no air conditioning. 105 degrees, sweltering, and the only place to sit was near the open-air window. The sun was setting and beating upon us. It was pretty, but very hot. Sweat dripped down my face the whole evening.

I am taken by surprise at how delightful Billy is. He has a strong personality, he's attractive, and proud of his accomplishments. He is motivated and driven. What you see is what you get, he said, and I believed him. He was outspoken, had liberal views, thirteen and a half years sober, and a *servant* at his church. Now we are getting somewhere.

He is vocal about liking me and we click. This was all in between dinner and his watching the Mariners on TV that he was absolutely distracted by. They are doing well for the first time in twenty years. His enthusiasm encouraged the server to give him two free tickets for the next day's matinee. He invited me but I had plans and turned him down.

It was the trains that went by regularly interrupting our meal that annoyed me the most. Not to mention sweat dripping down our faces. Even so, this is the best I felt about anyone in a very, very long time.

Billy is proud to talk about the house he built on Rosario Beach, not far from Deception Pass in Island County. The view of Puget Sound is spectacular, and the photos of Billy's house looks like something from a fairy tale. It turns out that he and his wife planned to retire there. He was married for decades and divorced a few years ago. She got the Condo in the city, I got the vacation home on the Island, he told me. He's still working but had plans on retiring there.

Billy and I went on our second date. It was fun, but a little stressful. I'd agreed to head up north to meet him for an outdoor concert at the breathtakingly beautiful Anacortes Marina. It was on a Friday afternoon when I already had plans two hours south prior to our date. Traffic is so congested on I-5 I was two and a half hours in ninety-six-degree temperature in stop and go traffic trying to get there. I arrived an hour after the concert started but nothing Billy and I didn't expect.

Eventually I chilled out and we swing our hips to the band watching former Heart members doing decent renditions of Ann and Nancy Wilson's hits. It was a little annoying to hear what good friends Billy was with the drummer and lead guitarist as I have the suspicion he barely knew them but liked to name drop. Plus, as soon as I arrived, he started complaining about stupid things like this driver should not get away with parking there, his mother's boyfriend is not her boyfriend, he's a roommate trying to take advantage of her. That would be a concern of mine, too, but they've been together over twenty years, and we are here for a concert and a date, not a grump session. I do like that he's opening up to me, though.

The setting was lovely. Certainly, a little whining is no deal breaker. I'm maybe a little unnerved by all the traffic stress getting here. I just want to relax and get to know Billy better. I was glad when he gave me a lift in his late model Volvo to go for tea at the upscale Anthony's on the waterfront after the concert.

His car was amazingly spotless "black on black" and he was sure to point this out several times. I was glad to see he used hand sanitizer, these are pandemic days, and you can't be too careful. The fact that he carried refreshing breath mints was very cute, too. What I noticed was that I didn't get offered any hand sanitizer or breath mints. I get it that when you live by yourself, you're not in the habit of offering things to others, so again, no big deal. I am not too shy to ask, and those mints were delightful.

I was able to take care of a couple items I'd had in mind to begin to get to know Billy better. I made it a serious moment and intentionally put my hand on his knee leaning forward and looked him in the eye and said, do you want to be Facebook friends? Thus, an avenue into how he interacts with friends and family, what's important enough for him to post, and how many other women are liking the things he posts. He did not hesitate to share his last name and friended me on the spot.

In the process he kept having a female picture of some fifty-three-year-old beautiful blonde pop up. Embarrassing for him. No biggie to me. He asked if we should change our Facebook status to 'in a relationship'. I was flattered, it felt like he was my first boyfriend for as long as I can remember, but I responded, "let's see how it goes".

The second agenda item I had was what he desired in a relationship. He said, "the same as you". After getting out of a twenty-eight-year marriage four years ago, "friends and a L.T.R.". I found that he spelled out L.T.R. rather odd when speaking. He wants a long-term relationship; commitment without committing. I get that. Sort of.

Things are going well. As he chatters about himself on and on, I ask questions about his family. I later laid in bed questioning two distinctive issues. While I just hate the idea of picking him apart, ruling him out like all the rest…I am concerned why his twenty-eight-year-old daughter had moved out of state without telling him. Billy blames his mother, his child's grandmother, for nagging his daughter about him. Who moves out of state without telling their dad? They are not as close as I was led to believe during earlier discussions with him.

When he described separating from his wife it was all about how his ex and his daughter ganged up against him. Sounds like he moved out five years before he physically left. From his point of view, it was his wife and daughter against him. Sounds like he broke up with his daughter, too. Also, he's saying his daughter and his own mother have ganged up against him. I could be wrong. I have learned working in domestic violence that what an ex would say could be one's best teacher. Also, a flag to spot a domestic violence perpetrator can be seen in how they try to control their mothers, sisters, and daughters. I'm not saying Billy is a perpetrator. I'm questioning why the women in his life don't like him.

The other immediate flag I have is about his ninety-five-year-old mother and her ninety-five-year-old boyfriend/roommate both with dementia living alone. Turns out mom is a hoarder, "it's really bad" he told me, and moving to a nursing home or adult family home "she says is out of the question". Billy says their main bathroom sink is broken and he had to go to another floor to wash his hands when visiting this week.

Now, he's a carpenter by trait. Why is mom's sink broken and he not there fixing it? Perhaps it just happened and I'm being all kinds of judgmental. Who knows? I just know that he has a poor relationship with all three women in his life and they are the only family he has. Mom, daughter, and the ex-wife who died two weeks ago.

Billy is focused on his mom leaving her $800,000 house to his daughter rather than him. "She'll just sell it…". Billy refers to it as the house he grew up in and believes he should get to keep it. I find the fact that he has a house, and his daughter would be the beneficiary of her grandmother's house, to be exciting whether she decides to sell or keep it.

Billy is coming across egotistical. He seems to be creating the story about the boyfriend "she says he's her boyfriend, but how can she trust this guy she's only known for twenty years over my dad she was married to for …" and "I say he's just a roommate". Why is he unable to accept his mom having a boyfriend?

Perhaps Billy has difficulty with change. He is in a different mood than last time or on the phone. He quotes his mother as saying, "I can't live alone", as if that is so horrible. Humm. My behavioral health training is starting to notice some unhealthy mood and personality traits. Maybe I've been working in mental health too long, and I find most people to have some aspect of this or that disorder, but I do make it a point not to evaluate them really. I know if I was his mom, in my nineties with dementia, I'd be screaming to not live alone either. I'm wondering why he isn't intervening or even thinking in those terms. His focus is on the inheritance, not getting her the help she may need.

People with mental illness just seem normal to me. Exciting and fun. Perhaps it reminds me of dad? He was sometimes fun and there was seldom a dull moment growing up. Perhaps it is a mirror to my soul. It is me. I am attracted to the big loud personality with opinions you don't care to hear but I'll tell you anyway. Just don't disagree with me. Untreated alcoholism??? Borderline Personality? Bipolar? But...he's strong and cute and makes me feel protected, says Cinderella looking for her knight in shining armor.

Despite some flags I continue to text with Billy. We make plans for a third date. Now I'm letting him in further, taking a risk. I do really like him, flaws and all. We plan for Billy to come to my neighborhood to see the campground where I have a travel trailer on a small lake. This is better than bringing him to my home should things not work out and is sure to bring out the Boy Scout in him. We decided to go kayaking. He's skinny, healthy, and an athlete and has never kayaked, it's time he did. I am none of these things, but he seems to be impressed by my hair, my education, and my smile. He agrees to be there at 10:00 am the next day.

I arrived early and blew up the kayaks. I'm so nervous to go on a date in a bathing suit, but it's okay. I'll wear a sundress over it and only take it off should we go swimming afterward. I lather myself in sunscreen and get the Kayaks ready to load in my car to bring to the lake.

I have to say I was disappointed when he canceled at the last minute due to having a stiff neck. He says he's going out for a ride on his Harley and wishes I were there to massage his neck. When he returned home feeling better, I let him know I'd be at the campground all day and he was welcome to come out. We did not have to kayak. He said, "Ok, TY Karen".

So, I wait. And wait. And wait. He texts, "Are you

wet yet? LOL". Not yet, I reply. You coming? I asked two hours after he said "okay" and I thought he was on his way. "Probably not", he texts, "So much to do here". I guess I misunderstood his text. It pissed me off that he said okay then didn't come.

I let him know I was going to a meeting.

I'm getting mad at him and think his stiff neck is just an excuse. I admit the drive is a lot, but come on, I just did the two-hour round trip twice to your neighborhood. Make some effort here.

While I was at the meeting, he texted me that he's in MA and thought I should know. "MA?" I ask, Massachusetts? Maine? "Marijuana Anonymous" he texts. "Except I almost quit…then my ex-wife passed…".

Humm. He told me he is thirteen and a half years sober. He does the marijuana maintenance program. No wonder he carries the resentments and seems self-centered. I wait to respond until I can gather my thoughts.

"I have no problem with you smoking pot. But I do have a serious problem with me getting involved with someone who smokes weed. That is a deal breaker for me. I do encourage that should you get ninety days clean you get back in touch with me. Thank you for your honesty, it's been really fun".

"Could I still text you on occasion to see how you are", he responds.

"That's probably not a good idea", I text.

400 texts, two dates, and it's over before it begins. He was noticeably into superficial things, especially himself. I did like him and his "black on black" Volvo, though. Then there's the vacation home on the water I never got to see. Now I'm sounding superficial. I will go

back to loading up the kayaks and cleaning the car. Ah, poor me. Poor me. Pour me another drink. Diet Pepsi, please, and a meeting on the side.

So close to the fairy tale of the dude who is active, attentive, and even attractive. Someone who works for a living and whose company was enjoyable. Being checked out is the deal breaker. Lying about being clean is where I come from, not where I'm going.

40 LOVE IS BLIND – OCTOBER 2022

Last night I was streaming the third season of "Love Is Blind" and realized how much that show has in common with online dating. The two weeks of intense communication before you even meet. The risk of opening your soul to your potential life partner, all in the quest for love.

The show is entertaining because the five couples who take the big risk and agree to marry one another before meeting are so very certain they have met their match. Yet, when they meet, they are taken back. It's not who they expected. Unaware their imagination has taken them to fantasy land, they attempt to recreate their partners to be who they thought they were. The first two seasons were disappointing to watch. Even the few couples that actually married after a month of getting to know one another didn't make it through time.

In online dating it happens too. The chatting, the connecting, the risk of going deeper and deeper. The illusion that you've found the one…now all you must do is meet and live happily ever after. That meat and potatoes is the real deal, not the black stallion and type of romance found only in fairy tales.

I can see how people get swindled out of their fortunes while seeking love from cat phishers overseas. There is this fantasy that you have found true love, everlasting love. Isn't that what we all want? What lengths do we go to love and be loved!

Here is what I know to be true. I love God. I love the teaching of the Buddha. I love unity found in Fellowship. I love connecting with friends, animals, and music. I love being present. I love being still, exhaling, being silent. I love myself, flawed and all. I am more than a body having a spiritual experience. I am spirit having a human experience.

I found the love I have been looking for. I love and trust in my understanding of God, Universal Truths, Spiritual Principles, most 12-Step Programs, The Buddha, The Dharma, and some Sangha's. I love working with newcomers and helping the sick heal. I love working the Steps and living the Dharma. I love daily 10th Steps and the 4th Noble Truth as they keep me in touch with where I am and where I am going.

I have found my strengths and areas I need to work on. I have felt spirit work through me and as me. At times I know I am part of the larger Universal Spirit. I am love. And love is all there is.

41 CRAVING – NOVEMBER 2022

As much as I am having an adverse reaction to dating most men on these dating sites, I crave getting that companion to complete me. Intellectually I know both are extreme and it is in the craving and aversion that causes my suffering.

Last night I participated in an online event with one of the Buddhist teachers, Ayya Dhammadipa. She spoke on the conundrum of craving. I enjoyed it so much I woke up seeking more (no craving there!). Today, I listened to a talk on accessing the intuitive. Both experiences got me out of my mind and into that sixth sense, the spiritual realm. More aware. Less body, more knowing. I'm on a spiritual path of belonging.

I do know that the recent MeetMindful.com messages from two David's and a John offer Mara, not companionship. Mara is the tease, the evil, the devil in disguise, the tempter. Both David's are a different age and location than their profiles. Easy to tell they are cat phishing and not who they say they are. Though it's hard to accept looking at their gorgeous GQ faces. John appeared to be real, still an hour and a half away from me, making it hard to meet. He sent me several very long and personal messages and moved the conversation from the dating site to email. When I suggested meeting and we exchanged more photos, he stopped responding.

As much as I know better, the dukkha sets in. The suffering. *Why did I send that one photo, the unflattering one? Was I too pushy, too forward? What was it that made him ghost me?* Today I sent the one last message attempt, John, are you still there?

These thoughts aren't even true. John may not be John. He may like the unflattering photo. He may have another interest. He could have died. Billions of reasons my reasoning is not based on reality. Who am I to understand, to beat myself up, to feel rejected for good or not so good reasons? I absolutely hate doing this to others and feeling it myself. It is the exact opposite of my intention. (Unless he responds, ha-ha), I'm really done now. No more dating sites. No seeking companions or lovers or imaginary friends. It is or it isn't. I'm choosing to be 100% satisfied with just me and my inner spirit, aka Great Spirit. Icing on the cake is my dogs but they are impermanent, too. I'm learning that everything is impermanent. Acceptance of this is key to happiness.

A very close friend of mine in Florida died. I am so sad. It's okay, too. Frontal lobe dementia. The angel in my life. She keeps showing up in music all around me. Love, love, love her.

These two talks on craving and on an intuitive mind inspired me to rise above. Starting with what I know. To understand my mind, I must understand my body. When I feel my feet and become conscious of pain, pleasure, and neutral states from my feet to my crown, I awaken to

Single and Sober: Who Found My Slipper?
feelings and emotions. Where I wear feelings that cling to my body I notice and move on, I don't cling to the pain or the pleasure. I notice the neutral states. I become more aware of my response to the different feeling tones and train my mind not to stay on the hamster wheel of having to have or having to avoid. Freedom is letting go of the craving.

The intuitive mind is curious. First, I notice there is no elephant in my living room. Here I am in physical form with my two dogs and a laptop. Rising above, I notice my feet. My mind is connected to my feet and the energy it takes to lift them with each step.

I am part of the forest. It's not just me and my dogs. My neighborhood, this forest, we are part of one. Call it one power, a higher power, the Creator, the Universe or the Galaxies. It is bigger than me and what I've come to trust.

When I meditate, I often rise above. Practicing the Metta helps me go there. I pray for my well-being, the well-being of my best buddy, for the health and happiness of a stranger, and finally, I wish the very best for my enemy. Love is always the answer.

As I mentioned earlier in this book, one time I was practicing Metta I realized that the anger I had toward someone in my life was standing in the way of world peace. I was blocking world peace by holding on to that anger. That was a light bulb moment for me. I can get out of the way, and I can let it go. For me, for them, for Unity and for love to exist in the Universe I have to surrender the hate. The only thing that stands in the way is my ego.

After practicing Metta I feel connected to the greater good of world peace. Intuitively, I rise out of my setting, my building, the limitation of my body. In spirit and using visualization, I reach my hands out to other people and we breathe as if we are one. We send light and love through our bodies, to the room, the building, the neighborhood, the city, the county, and across the state. We send light and love across the United States and over the seven continents. I am sure to spread extra love to the places where people I know reside, like Hawaii, Michigan, and Florida. I am holding hands with other people surrounding the globe and our feet work in sync to spin the globe behind us until every country, every remote island, every being on this earth feels the love. Love is all there is.

The Buddha's Four Noble Truths lay the foundation. Suffering exists; it sucks to be sick, grow old, be lonely, grieve, etc., etc., etc. This is the first arrow. When I quit resisting this fact my expectations begin to ease. If I recognize I can react to these disturbances positively or negatively, I can at least control not adding to my suffering and shooting a second arrow.

The cause of all suffering is craving; wishing I had something I don't have or not wanting to let go of something I have, clinging. I can only relax when I let go and accept what I can and can't control. I need to remain neutral and right sized in the face of adversity and know a power exists larger than I. Peace, serenity, and contentment are in my heart. As is, right here and right now.

Ayya shared a Japanese poem this morning during her talk, once a haiku prior to translation. "The thief left behind the moon out the window". That first arrow of suffering can take my things, but nothing can touch that larger spirit to which I am connected to the Universe. Only if I shoot myself with a second arrow in my reaction can I disconnect from my higher power, thus, create more suffering for myself and those around me.

42 READY TO RETIRE – FEBRUARY 2023

I'm sixty-three now, making future plans; when to retire, where to retire, how to use my assets, and I'm not even thinking about if I will or won't have a partner. I'm okay as is. I understand that I'm not by myself for lack of trying and I'm not by myself.

I know I'm not alone. My spirit is connected to a higher energy, love, power, God, I don't even care anymore what it's called. Although I still have an iota of wince when it's given a male gender identity.

My work is fulfilling as a Behavioral Health Specialist in a Medical Clinic serving uninsured, underinsured, Medicaid, and Medicare patients. Most days I feel like a vehicle of something much larger, I know I'm still of use in society. My patients let me know they benefit from my work with them. I benefit from their work with me. Other days my ego sets in, and I wonder if I'm too cynical and burnt out to continue this path. I will not miss getting reamed out by patients who feel miserable and want to be sure I feel that way too before they leave my office. Fortunately, they are rare.

I love the Buddha's teaching of a monk pouring his student a cup of tea. I paraphrase. The teacup fills up and begins to spill over. The monk continues to pour. The student looks confused. The monk explains the student must be ready for new information to be received or the teacher wastes their time.

I continue to go to 12-Step meetings every chance I get and spend time with my animals when I'm not at a support group. I am grateful for meetings in person again since the covid epidemic started and is officially considered over now. That was a long three years without many meetings! It's tough to combat this disease without other recovering addicts or alcoholics. I had my tiny group of support people; we kept one another's spirits alive while meeting underground during that time. We took the risk of exposure to stay socially sane. I was blessed for all the zoom meeting options for my sobriety and for that of the newcomer. Still, I longed for more fellowship and meetings.

However, the Buddhist Recovery group is the one online virtual meeting I attended each week since the pandemic began. While I've grown through the lust I had with the facilitator, I see that the infatuation was simply my imagination clinging to something outside myself wanting to fill up my insides. The suffering ceased once I realized I was the cause.

Sponsee's have come back into my life. After three Sponsee's I worked with that had more than twenty years of recovery relapsed by excusing "just wine" or "just weed" or "just sick and [over] medicating", I took a break from sponsoring women just before covid hit. I was hurt by the years of lying, not so much the relapses.

After a couple years of down time, the powers that be saw fit that I had something to offer others; my experience, strength, and hope to never have to use again. I was sent a few women my way. They keep me enthused, on fire for my recovery, and grateful for having several decades clean and sober. I hope to never forget not being able to get thirty days, and to always appreciate thirty plus years off alcohol and other drugs. Hope and being part of something bigger continue to fuel my journey. Left to my own devices, I'd be a hopeless dope fiend. Instead, I'm a dope less hope fiend.

I decided to step up to the plate in my home group and take on the Group Service Representative (GSR) position (and treasurer, secretary, coin person, and sometimes the chairperson). As a result, I'm learning more about the grown-up fellowship's way of conducting business. I'm impressed and amazed by how these groups of once sick, overly opinionated, rigid thinkers can get so much done and spread the message of hope and freedom from alcoholism and other addictions across the globe. I am truly blessed to be present for my life and part of this amazing movement.

43 SIXTY-FOUR & SO MUCH MORE – NOVEMBER 2023

I am an old woman now at sixty-four and loving every minute of it. I still wear combat boots, tight jeans, and cool ponchos. I plan to live to the average age of women in the US, eighty-eight. By this calculation, I have twenty-four more years to invest in my future, only I'm not clinging or averting to things these days. This will always be plan B and what happens will be plan A.

I'm simply watching feelings come and go. Just because I have a feeling doesn't mean I have to act on it. Just because I have a thought doesn't mean it's true. Just for today, I never have to use alcohol, other drugs, toxic food, people, or gambling to change the way I feel. I am happy, joyous, and free of this whack-a-mole brain. Just for today I have thirty-one years clean and sober, but I recognize that according to AA I am "not cured of alcoholism. What [I] really have is a daily reprieve contingent on the maintenance of [my] spiritual program".

Thanks for joining me as I share my story. I am

happy, joyous, and free from active addiction, craving dopamine, adrenaline, and having to have a man to be complete. I am enough.

I found my slipper.

UPDATE – FEBRUARY 29, 2024

Americans are often faced with a dilemma when they get ready to retire. Either they have been able to save their 401(3)Bs to help sustain their lifestyle when they stop working or they try to live off 25% of their working income which can be the case at retirement. Or they have nothing saved and are SOL. For me, I'm somewhere in the middle.

Some retirees have families that help the seniors in their home or community, too. That is not a value in my European Irish culture of this era or in my neighborhood where I reside alone in my single-family home. My neighbors are not trained to observe and do not help with trash or gardening. However, I can occasionally ask someone to turn off my water when a pipe bursts, something I am grateful for as I lose my strength to handle certain home repair needs. I hire out for help with gardening and while I love my gardeners, I cannot afford to keep up this home or my yard for much longer.

I watch those around me, and it seems there are the haves and the have not groups. People who have often are healthy and have more than one social security income and/or pensions. In my case I've never been married, used a bit of my retirement to invest in some housing opportunities, but I don't have enough money to live comfortably when I stop working unless I make some major lifestyle changes.

I could not afford to live independently in the Seattle area on the meager SSI I have earned after working for fifty years, even with three college degrees. It does pay to be a white male who can earn a living wage or to pick a man's career. At eighteen years of age my son could earn more money than I without training or an education.

Most social workers can barely pay back student loans. There is some help available after ten years if you work for a non-profit or government agency, usually making low wages. I didn't know while in college that my career would be entirely at non-profit agencies, or I would have taken loans instead of being a starving student. My child ate good, but we qualified for food stamps.

I took no student loans knowing the field I was entering paid women's wages. It helped to have subsidized housing as I moved from minimum wage to college student, and then to give up the HUD voucher to become a first-time homeowner. I bought a home for my graduation present and raised my son without moving homes again from the time he was in the fifth grade on. Prior to that I moved every two years or more often from 1970 to 2001. It's been nice to live in the same house for the past twenty-three years and offer my son a new way of life.

I took a trip a couple years ago to Puerto Vallarta, Mexico. Prior to the pandemic it was the American Dream to retire there. The cost of living, prescriptions, medical care, and especially housing was so attractive people were bursting at the seams to move. I visited toward the end of the pandemic and found the prices to be higher than I expected as the community tried to recover from years without travelers. While housing was more affordable, the infrastructure had problems. Running water, toilets, and showering was scarcer. The people were wonderful. There was a lot of tolerance for what seemed like wealthy American tourists that didn't speak or try to speak the language.

Effort was made by so many natives to communicate and there seemed to be an expectation by the American tourists for the Mexican people to appreciate every single peso left as a tip. I was curious about what it would be like to retire there, but unsure due to some basic safety concerns about doing this without a partner. At times I was embarrassed to be an American tourist there.

My father taught me how to haggle, though, that part was rather fun. My son was the real natural, though. He seldom passed a math class in school but could haggle better than all the tourists put together. His math skills became brilliant under the right circumstances. Where he got the confidence to go with it is beyond me.

A few years ago, I bought a membership into a camping club in WA state with the idea of living there in a travel trailer during the summer and going somewhere else for the winter once I retired. I wondered if Mexico in the winter would make sense, but I was too apprehensive to have this as a plan to do alone. The park where I purchased a camping club membership is in Lake Stevens, WA. The campground has a small private lake, Lake Connor, and is surrounded by the Cascade Mountains. It is a family's summer vacation haven with three clubhouses, loads of excitement all summer including live bands playing old peoples rock-n-roll, activities on the calendar most of the year, and children driving around in golf carts.

Single and Sober: Who Found My Slipper?

The law in this county prohibits living there all year but allows six months of occupancy. I'm told this is so there are no property taxes on temporary campground land making it more affordable. My past few summers have been a blast, though I've been living in my home and just visiting the park on long weekends. The park sells food, offers music on the weekends, and a couple of pools I use regularly. It has a nice, friendly, vacation feel.

Last year, I learned of a membership available with a large RV for sale in another park on the other side of Snohomish County. This campground is on Tulalip Tribal land with access not only to the multiple pools and a gym, but with beach access to Puget Sound where I could run my dogs. Because I would like to retire before the end of this year, I took the leap and bought a membership in the park at a site with a thirty-three-foot trailer instead of eighteen feet like at Lake Connor.

This trailer has a pop-out giving it the sense of an extra room and feels more like a tiny house. It has also been covered with a thirty-foot covered deck and roof add on since it was almost new. Located only thirteen miles from my house, it has become my happy place. Here it feels more like a little house in a small town, with 2500 lots spread out over 800 wooded acres, it has a store, post office, laundromat, including family and adult centers for gathering. My retirement plan is starting to come together.

My three bedroom, two and a half bath home in Marysville has served me well. I could sell it, rent it, or stay living in it. In the twenty+ years I've owned it, I've done a couple of refinances, but gotten the interest rate and payment low. I would like to leave it to my adult son when I die. He probably won't live in it, but he could benefit from my lifelong process of buying and maintaining it. Even if he sells it this fulfills my wish to leave the next generation better off. I am privileged to be a property owner and other than my son, it is my prize possession. Not that my son is my property. He is my gift from God.

I am a sucker for helping people, for picking unreliable renters, and falling for a sob story. As history proves, I cannot be responsible for picking good tenants or dealing with their pleas to postpone rent, etc. As a result, I have checked into property management outfits and learned what it would take to get my house ready for renters and for them to take over finding good tenants. Now, I sit here wondering if I can really do it. Can I willingly get rid of a lifetime of collecting things and move into eighteen to thirty-three feet of travel trailers?

I love my sister's take on it. You can always change your mind. It's so simple, and so true. My house will rent for a lot more money than my mortgage payment, my bills at the campgrounds will be minimal, and most of all my campground expenses will be covered by what the renters pay. Hopefully the rental will allow for putting a percentage of the income into a home repair program and a tax fund if needed. I will have enough money and time to travel. I may become a traveling slumlord, but I will keep up the property maintenance.

Ah, the guilt. I sometimes would prefer having unhoused people take residence. It's simply not practical, though. I could sell, but then I'd waste my life's investment money most likely and leave nothing behind. There is something to be said about helping the next generation. Not so much to make them greedy, but it takes generations to accumulate wealth and my upbringing did not allow me this nor teach me how to not live in poverty.

I want to say my desire to downsize is there, but so is my greed and spoiled lifestyle filled with craving. I want to live in a campground most of the time, but I imagine I'll want to go home sometimes, too. I haven't lived at either campground for more than a week, it's hard to tell if six months here and there is going to work for me. Even if I do it for two to five years it would allow me to stop working this year, which I long for, and to lighten my load.

What I love about my plan is retiring and waiting to collect social security for as long as I can. The difference between collecting social security at sixty-five and seventy is tremendous. I can get Medicare at sixty-five, thus, I could stop working this fall, and I plan to. Since I expect to live until eighty-eight, I want the seventy-year social security rate, it only makes sense. Now, can I hold out in the woods by myself with my higher power, my laptop, and my doggies?

All my life I've been waiting to not have to get up and work for the man. While I'm making more money today than I have ever earned in this lifetime, and I enjoy making a living wage finally, I am eager to stop working. I've listened to enough sadness and people in pain as a Behavioral Health therapist for a lifetime. Prior to this job I worked in suicide prevention. Before that I worked with pregnant and post-partum women and their children. There is nothing more satisfying than helping two generations find sobriety and health. However, I am tired.

I do enjoy it some days still, and I feel the impact I have on people's lives, but I can keep helping through my 12-Step community. Having one sponsee is different than having over a hundred twenty-five patients a month. I look forward to helping without having it suck the life out of me. I could always hang a shingle somewhere and just work part-time as I wish, though it's not likely. I am tired of working. In two to five years, I will most likely return to larger living quarters than at the campgrounds, but I'll hopefully have an income proportionate to do so when I move back out of the woods. I have no idea how most seniors make ends meet and survive.

Travel with me on this journey toward retirement. My plan is to give a two month notice in July as is expected, get health insurance in September, and quit working ASAP this fall. I have only a little retirement money left after buying these campground memberships and travel trailers, so packing up, selling my pile, and giving away my lifelong treasures is in short order. This will be a year of change. I have no doubt I'll be kicking and screaming throughout, reminding myself I can always change my mind and using Marie Kondo videos to bless my possessions and let them go. Wish me luck!

Keep an eye out for my next memoir: "Sixty-four and So Much More".

Sign up for my newsletter for updates at www.KarenFoleyWriter.com. If you haven't done so already.

PS: If anyone can figure out how to hook up and use this travel trailer toilet, I'd be much obliged. My sh-- doesn't stink, honest, LOL. The black sewer line is my current challenge. I know I can learn; I also know I don't want to know.

Both campgrounds have nearby bathhouses. I'll be fine.

Single and Sober: Who Found My Slipper?

ABOUT THE AUTHOR

Meet Karen Foley, LICSW, MSW, SUDP, the compassionate voice behind the transformative book: "Single and Sober: Who Found My Slipper?" and the short story "I Thought I Would Die". With over three decades of experience in the treatment field, Karen's passion shines through as she guides recovering alcoholics, addicts, and their loved ones on the path to understanding addiction and embracing recovery through the lens of lived experience.

Drawing from her extensive professional background and personal journey, Karen's writing resonates with authenticity and empathy. She intimately knows the challenges of addiction, having experienced its grip firsthand, yet she also celebrates the freedom and joy of over 30 years of active recovery.

Through her books and speaking engagements, Karen fosters connection and hope, illuminating the often tumultuous yet ultimately rewarding journey toward sobriety. For those seeking guidance or insight into the world of addiction and recovery, Karen Foley offers a beacon of support and understanding.

Stay connected with Karen and explore her latest work by visiting her website and signing up for her newsletter: www.KarenFoleyWriter.com.

DISCLOSURE

Names have been changed of the people to protect confidentiality. Permission was granted by some of the characters discussed. Effort to contact others was made when practical. Stories you read are only from the author's perspective. It is likely each person would have their own tale to tell, and it would look different than the authors.

The author is not an authority in any 12-Step program, Buddhism, or Buddhist Recovery Practice. She hopes to share her experience to help others see that recovery is possible.

Many of the words and thoughts that are expressed in this book are not unique to the author. They are a culmination of spending endless hours in meetings, practicing the 12-Steps, Buddhism, and osmosis from the wisdom of the fellowship. It is inevitable that after 30 plus years of regular meeting attendance in 12-Step rooms that include NA, AA, OA, GA, Nic-Anon, and Buddhist Recovery Meetings the literature has been recited.

Many thanks to Alcoholics Anonymous "Big Book", Narcotics Anonymous "Basic Text", and Gambler's Anonymous "Yellow Book" for influencing both this book and the authors' perspective. I am indebted to the predecessors that came before me for teaching me how to grow and become part of the unity found in the fellowship. If you are reading this book and sick and tired of being sick and tired; go to a meeting, get a sponsor, find a higher power, and commit to attending a home group. Work the Steps, then pay it forward. Your quality of life will forever be uplifted and you, too, can live a life beyond your wildest dreams. Find your slipper. Peace. Be still.

WORKS CITED

Alcoholics Anonymous, AA Big Book app; Second Edition. 1955. Pg. 66/67/85.

Browne, Jackson. "The Pretender" 1976. The Pretender. 1979.

Byars Beckwith, Rickie. "Use Me" 1993. I Found a Deeper Love. https://m.youtube.com/playlist/.

Cook, Sam. "Another Saturday Night". Ain't That Good News. 1963/Cat Stevens. Home in the Sky. 1974.

Denver, John. "Leaving on a Jet Plane" 1966. Rhymes & Reasons 1969. "Annie's Song" 1973. Back Home Again 1974.

Dhammadipa, Ayya. "Conundrum of Craving". November 2022.

Griffin, Kevin. "One Breathe at a Time: Buddhism and The Twelve Steps". 2004.

Love Is Blind - Season 3. October 19-November 9, 2022. Dallas, TX.

Mac, Fleetwood. "Landslide" 1975. Stevie Nicks. Fleetwood Mac 1975.

Mitchell, Joni. "River" 1971. Blue 1971.

Narcotics Anonymous, NA White Booklet, How It Works. 1976. Pg 5.

Nicks, Stevie. Don Henley. "Leather and Lace" 1981. Bella Donna. 1981.

Ochs, Phil. "Love Me I'm a Liberal" 1966. Phil Ochs In Concert 1966.

Petty, Tom and the Heartbreakers. "The Waiting"1981. Hard Promises. 1981.

Stevens, Cat. Aka Yusuf Islam. "On The Road to Find Out", Tea for the Tillerman. 1970.